"I had no idea that God would use Randy Pope to establish a spiritual colossus. He qualifies as a role model and mentor to all pastors. He has designed this book to be a catalyst for more effectively doing the work of the ministry. I applaud the centrality of evangelism in the church's program."

Dr. John Edmund Haggai
Founder and Chairman, Haggai Institute

"To those who long for guidance, here are seeds of destiny. What a gift! I wish that every starting and striving pastor I know would plunge into these chapters—they would emerge exhilarated."

Carl George
Consulting for Growth, Diamond Bar, California

"I have known Randy Pope for more than twenty years, and what he has written in *The Intentional Church* is an inviting expression of the passion that is the signature of his life and ministry. . . . In this book, Randy has given the Church a refreshing, creative, biblical approach that rescues us from the rut of just 'doing church.' . . . This book is an invigorating breath of fresh air!"

Dr. Crawford W. Loritts Jr.
Speaker, Author, Radio Host
Associate Director, Campus Crusade for Christ USA

"Wow! A practical and profound book on ministry design that isn't so complicated that only a genius could understand it or so superficial and shallow that nobody would want to. This is a book that ought to be in the hands of every pastor who loves the church and wants to see the church shatter the gates of hell. Randy Pope has been there, done that, and has the T-shirt. If you're a pastor and you miss this one, you ought to go into vinyl repair."

Steve Brown
Professor of Preaching at Reformed Theological Seminary
Bible Teacher, Key Life

"*The Intentional Church* is not a theoretical book. Randy Pope lives and practices what he preaches. This book should be an inspiration to every church leader who is willing to be open to God's vision."
Dr. Michael Youssef
Founding Rector
The Church of the Apostles

"It is said that 'good fruit' is evidence of a good root. I have seen first-hand the 'fruit' of Randy Pope's ministry in the changed lives of his church members, the healthy growth of his church and the authenticity of his life and leadership. Now Randy desires to help every church and church leader make sure they are having fruit in their own ministry . . . fruit that remains!"
Dr. Bob Reccord
President, Southern Baptist North American Mission Board

"I know of no one better than Randy Pope at thinking strategically about church ministry—and especially about evangelism. His lifelong effectiveness and achievement as the pastor of Perimeter Church and its network attests to this. This book distills Randy's considerable wisdom about these subjects into a very readable volume."
Tim Keller
Senior Pastor, Redeemer Presbyterian Church
New York, New York

"With the experience of a seasoned servant-warrior, the wisdom which can only come with tears and scars, the helpful applications of a faithful practitioner, Randy Pope has given us his heart, and not just an outstanding book on the church. Who needs this book? Pastors like me who need to be reminded of the things which mean the most to the heart of God. Congregations like mine, which too easily can become consumer driven, rather than being consumed with the glory and grace of Jesus Christ."
Scotty Smith,
Senior Pastor, Christ Community Church,
Franklin, Tennessee

"I've watched Randy Pope for over twenty years, as he has emerged into ministry beginning with nothing but a devoted wife and commitment to reach a community for Christ. I've seen him innovate, hone and execute multiple strategies, testing them to see which ones stood the test of time. This book is the fruit of that labor. Randy has been used of God to build one of the finest churches in America —a thoughtful, powerful, relational, evangelistic, assimilating, multiplying and kingdom impact church. He shares his strategy in this book with clarity and practical tools for empowerment. Catch his heart and the heart of his church and it will rock your world. May his tribe increase!"

Dr. Ron Jenson
Chairman, Future Achievement International
San Diego, California

"Randy Pope is a man of extraordinary vision for the church. Just being around him awhile you know that he's an extremely gifted leader. It is a blessing for the kingdom that he has used his vision and leadership gifts to have such an impact on Perimeter Church and Perimeter's ministries. His insight will challenge you and stretch your vision. It will help you to dream dreams for your ministry and local church."

G. Bryant Wright
Senior Pastor, Johnson Ferry Baptist Church

"Randy Pope is one of the most gifted and creative ministers I know. For years he has been doing seminars for pastors on how to build a prevailing church. Now he has put his principles in book form making this powerful material available on a broad scale. Here are the principles that have resulted in reaching the unchurched and developing mature, reproducing disciples!"

Frank M. Barker, Jr.
Pastor Emeritus, Briarwood Presbyterian Church
Birmingham, Alabama

"When I'm asked to list significant church leaders in 21st century America, the name Randy Pope is one I always include. With God's blessing, Perimeter has built a church culture that is uniquely equipped to reach people for Christ in our post-modern world. In *The Intentional Church*, Randy Pope lays out the principles and practicalities that have produced such an effective work for God. If your goal is to build a powerful church for Christ, then this is your book!"

> Lon Solomon
> Senior Pastor, McLean Bible Church
> McLean, Virginia

"I wish I had this book when I began pastoring churches. Congregations, laymen and pastors will profit by examining how Randy Pope implemented biblical principles of developing lay leadership of ministry at all levels of the church. At Perimeter Church, Randy is not a one man gang. Instead he has a large gang of trained lay people doing the work of the ministry."

> Dr. Jim Baird
> Pastor Emeritus, First Presbyterian Church
> Jackson, Mississippi
> Dean of Chapel, Belhaven College
> Director of Church Relations
> Reformed Theological Seminar, Jackson, Mississippi

"If anyone knows how to do church, it's Randy Pope . . . and with excellence! I highly recommend *The Intentional Church*, a timely and transforming book filled with practical jewels that will enrich every ministry."

> Dr. Robert M. Lewis
> Teaching Pastor, Fellowship Bible Church
> Little Rock, Arkansas

The
Intentional
Church

*Moving from Church Success
to Community Transformation*

REVISED AND UPDATED

Randy Pope

MOODY PUBLISHERS
CHICAGO

All Scripture quotations, unless otherwise indicated, are taken from the *New American Standard Bible®*, Copyright © The Lockman Foundation 1960, 1962, 1963, 1968, 1971, 1972, 1973, 1975, 1977, 1995. Used by permission.

Scripture quotations marked NASB 1977 are taken from the *New American Standard Bible®*, Copyright © The Lockman Foundation 1960, 1962, 1963, 1968, 1971, 1972, 1973, 1975, 1977. Used by permission.

Scripture quotations marked NIV are taken from the *Holy Bible, New International Version®*. NIV®. Copyright © 1973, 1978, 1984 by International Bible Society. Used by permission of Zondervan Publishing House. All rights reserved.

Scripture quotations marked NLT are taken from the *Holy Bible, New Living Translation*, copyright © 1996. Used by permission of Tyndale House Publishers, Inc., Wheaton Illinois 60189, U.S.A. All rights reserved.

Scripture quotations marked KJV are taken from the King James Version.

Scripture quotations marked NRSV are from the *New Revised Standard Version* of the Bible, copyright 1946, 1952, and 1971 by the Division of Christian Education of the National Council of the Churches of Christ in the USA. Used by permission. All rights reserved.

Cover Designer: Smartt Guys Design
Cover Image: Jean Louis Batt / Getty Images
Editor: Jim Vincent

Library of Congress Cataloging-in-Publication Data

Pope, Randy.
  The intentional church : moving from church success to community transformation / Randy Pope.— Rev. and updated.
     p. cm.
  Rev. ed. of: The prevailing church. c2002.
  Includes bibliographical references.
   ISBN-13: 978-0-8024-2740-3
   1. Pastoral theology. 2. Church growth. I. Pope, Randy. Prevailing church. II. Title.

BV4011.3.P67 2006
253—dc22

                                                              2005032114

We hope you enjoy this book from Moody Publishers. Our goal is to provide high-quality, thought-provoking books and products that connect truth to your real needs and challenges. For more information on other books and products written and produced from a biblical perspective, go to www.moodypublishers.com or write to:

Moody Publishers
820 N. LaSalle Boulevard
Chicago, IL 60610

ISBN: 0-8024-2740-5
ISBN-13: 978-0-8024-2740-3

1 3 5 7 9 10 8 6 4 2

Printed in the United States of America

*Dedicated to my two families
who have loved me unconditionally
throughout these many years:*

*Carol, Matt, Rachael, Dena, and David,
who have made my personal life a daily joy;*

*and the people of Perimeter Church, who have
patiently endured enough mistakes, weaknesses, and failures
to eventually emerge as a church that prevails*

Contents

Foreword

TO THE FIRST EDITION

When Randy Pope asked me to write the foreword to *The Prevailing Church*, I was struck by the thought of how the work he launched in 1977, Perimeter Church, has been just that: *prevailing*.

This book is the story and ministry philosophy of Perimeter Church. Starting with a few dollars and no core group, Randy and his wife, Carol, set out on a journey which has taken them from "victory unto victory" with all the in-between struggles, hurts, and growing pains associated with forward thinking ministries. Through twenty-five years of societal change, economic ups and downs, and spiritual formations, Perimeter Church has been and is *prevailing*.

Randy Pope is faithful and innovative. In a very quiet and systematic manner, he has led Perimeter to become a model church in evangelism, discipleship, and leadership development—all of which are very dear to my heart.

Because of Randy's tenacious faithfulness and others following his example over the years, Perimeter has grown mightily in influence in Atlanta and beyond. He has led Perimeter in planting over twenty-five churches in the sprawling Altanta area. Under his leadership, Perimeter has designed a unique approach to Christian schooling, becoming a model to new schools around the country, and has begun church planting centers in nine countries, responsible for planting several hundred churches internationally.

Few congregations across the country have the benefit of a long tenured, founding pastor like Randy, with such a passion for the lost. Those who do tend to be prevailing churches.

The Prevailing Church is a relevant resource whether you are a pastor or layperson. Within it you'll find not only the amazing story of an innovative leader and congregation, but more importantly, a design for ministry that models unselfishness, generosity, and passion for people to savingly experience Jesus Christ.

John C. Maxwell
Founder, The INJOY Group

Acknowledgments
TO THE FIRST EDITION

Many thanks are in order to my wife, Carol, and our kids for their willingness to give away their husband and dad for two weeks each summer for four years so that I could write this book.

Thank you, Rob Reichel, for securing a spot for me to write in Hilton Head, South Carolina, each of those summers. And a special thanks to Hilton Head residents David and Kathy Brown and Robert and Manelle Graves for allowing me to use their homes when they were gone to do all this writing. I am greatly indebted to Neil Wilson, who did an outstanding job of editing this work, and to my secretary, Jackie Lucas, for the hours she spent preparing my manuscript, getting it ready for the publisher. And speaking of publishers, I am so grateful for the many gracious people I have gotten to know at Moody, especially Jim Bell, Senior Editor, with whom I have worked closely.

And last, but not least, thanks to the staff of Perimeter Church, who labored diligently with me, experimenting with ideas to see what worked; to our elders, who encouraged me to write and have lovingly shepherded me consistently; and to our church members, who have been willing "to attempt things doomed to failure unless God be in them."

May these thoughts and shared experiences, in some small way, benefit the King and His kingdom to whom I owe my all.

To God be the glory.

Introduction

WHAT WILL IT TAKE TO BE TRULY SUCCESSFUL?

You have picked up this book for reasons that are unknown to me. You may be looking for something that will energize your ministry. How many times have we looked for some fresh idea that might truly help us have greater success? Often our experience falls short of the success that others have experienced and we move to the next "new" program or product.

It is natural to want our ministries to succeed. However, as I have engaged in conversations with pastors and leaders in the church, I am struck with how many of them are weary from pursuing bigger budgets, building bigger staffs, and building bigger congregations. Certainly achieving these things reflects success to some degree, but I wonder if you are where I am—wondering whether these things measure the kind of success that truly transforms people, communities, or the world.

As I was growing up, my only experience with church was with

......that played it safe and stayed away from controversy. These churches did not think in the realm of success or failure because they rarely strayed outside of their comfort zones. They did not expect much from the people within their fellowship beyond their own ministries within the church. I had never known a pastor I could admire as a man's man. Indeed if I had met such a leader, I would have seriously questioned why he would give himself to such a feeble cause.

I have come to describe such churches as *precautionary*. That's a word we don't hear very often; it's the adjective for the word *precaution* and means "taking necessary measure against possible danger, harm or failure." Such bodies are lifeless, powerless, visionless . . . defeated.

But Jesus wants so much more for His church!

Eventually His Son proved more attractive to me than His would-be representatives in my early life, and I became a follower of Christ. Early in my spiritual pilgrimage as a new believer, I was introduced to churches that shattered my previous image of the bride of Christ. And I fell in love with God's church.

In those churches I met people who saw themselves, not as a make-no-waves service organization, but as a wartime army engaged in battle. Within their often-ordinary lives they displayed a remarkable sense of purpose. They were serious about their faith—but not self-righteous. They were comfortable with spiritual warfare terminology—without casting themselves as heroes for Christ. Their singular passion was to follow the Lord. Their attitude was contagious! I wanted to be like them, lead like them, serve like them. In those early years these leaders modeled the value of having big visions, hard visions, and noble visions. I have seen our people at Perimeter respond time and time again to visions that other churches would have dismissed as just too big.

Originally published as *The Prevailing Church, The Intentional Church* has been updated to provide examples of how applying these principles has led to significant changes at Perimeter.

I have chosen to wait beyond my first quarter-century of pastoring a church before writing on this subject. The passage of time allows me to assess the effectiveness of rightly understanding and implementing the principles that I describe in this book. However, as I write I am somewhat tentative—not because I don't feel strongly about these principles, but rather because I do feel so strongly.

Some of my tentativeness comes as I realize that much of what I say describes my individual experience and may not easily apply universally. I also know that some of what you will read in these pages will be misunderstood even though it represents what I believe to be an accurate description of biblical principles. It also breaks many long-accepted and seldom-questioned "rules" about God's design for the church. I am convinced that the principles of the transformational church run contrary to the current measures of success such as attendance, budget, and staff size.

In writing this, I also live with the realization that some of what I am writing about will have changed by the time you read this. I tell you these things at the outset because although our church has thought long and hard about structure and design, in the final analysis so much of what we do is organic in nature. Our church grows, ages, changes, learns, adapts, and continually seeks to become more like what her Lord intends her to be. Yes, many of the details will have changed by the time you read these words, but the core will remain. The principles you are about to consider in these pages will look different when you begin to apply them in your church and in the community that God has called you to serve.

So it is with much humility that I share with you the story of my particular corner of God's church, Perimeter Church in Atlanta, Georgia. We have learned some things in our journey as a fellowship that I believe might be helpful. You should not think of Perimeter as some model superchurch. I love Perimeter Church as none other, but like a parent with his or her children, I know better than anyone the flaws that exist.

Were you to move to Atlanta and join Perimeter, I would hope and expect that you would love her too. But only then would you see how flawed the ministry is, and how many opportunities we have to beautify this portion of Christ's bride. I suppose that those opportunities are a big part of what has kept me pastoring this church these many years. Any success we have is due to *being an intentional church,* with a ministry plan adopted after much prayer, discussion, and significantly, the leading of the Holy Spirit.

It is not my desire to replicate little "Perimeter-like" churches all over the country. However, I would love to see God raise up churches all around the world who confidently understand God's calling for their fellowship, declaring that they will not be precautionary. They choose instead to become churches influencing those parts of the world in which they serve.

If you share with me this sense of excitement about being involved in the unique ministry that God has designed for your church, let me encourage you to press on with determination and urgency. My desire for you is that you will become an intentional church that increases in influence. I must warn you, however, that as we begin this journey together the path will seem deceptively easy, and you will be tempted to underestimate the impact that these simple principles can have in your church. But I make this promise to you. If you diligently work through each of these principles with your leadership team, you will experience a transformation that will allow you to take your ministry to a new place, a place of transformational influence.

We must rethink success and not be too quick to accept the definitions employed by so many today. Wherever you are, whatever you are seeking for your church, I invite you to explore with me a vision of becoming a church that can be used to transform the lives of your people, your surrounding community, and even the world, for the glory of God.

WHAT JESUS WANTS FROM HIS CHURCH

Imagine you have just moved into a new community and are looking for a church home. You ask around, call around, and drive around; you let your fingers do the walking through the Yellow Pages—and the clicking through the Internet. You know that you will likely visit several churches before finding one that seems to fit. What single descriptive term would you choose to best describe your ideal church community?

Biblically and doctrinally sound? Vibrant and worshipful? Warm and caring? Growing and dynamic? Family oriented?

Or you may be a church leader, whether lay or professional, wrestling with a vision for your church. You've been to the conferences and read the literature. Purpose-driven . . . seeker-sensitive . . . postmodern . . . emergent . . . you've heard them all. And what you really long for is a church that *matters,* a church that influences and impacts her people and her community for the glory of God and His kingdom.

You long for a transformational church.

This is the church Jesus had in mind: a place where God's power is demonstrated with such force in its people that the community it serves is marked with an indelible spiritual imprint, transforming the lives of worshipers and those whom they contact.

"BUT WHO DO YOU SAY I AM?"

The transformational church owes its vision to the words of its leader more than two thousand years ago. Jesus had taken His small band of followers into the district known as Caesarea Philippi. Perhaps while looking at the various shrines built on the nearby hillside to honor man-made gods, Jesus began to talk about public opinion. He may have first pointed to some of those idols and asked, "What do people really think about these gods?" That question would have certainly set the stage for what followed.

We join the discussion in time to hear Jesus ask the disciples, "Who do people say that the Son of Man is?" (Matthew 16:13). Interestingly, every name the men threw out was someone returned from the dead: John the Baptist, Elijah, Jeremiah, "or one of the prophets" (v. 14).

But Jesus was unconcerned with the "buzz" going around about His origins. He had no intention of building His church and ultimately conquering the world for His kingdom's sake through ill-informed crowds. He would carry out His mission through men and women just like these twelve followers.

So Jesus served up the significant question: "But who do you say that I am?" (v. 15). Peter, the unofficial and self-appointed leader of the disciples, was quick, as usual, to respond: "You are the Christ, the Son of the living God" (v. 16). His impulsive exclamation could not have been more precise!

Jesus let Peter know how blessed he was to be so accurate, making sure he also knew that only God the Father deserved the credit for giving him such insight and understanding (v. 17). Peter was probably nodding his head in agreement when Jesus said something that caught him completely off guard: "I also say to you that you are Peter, and upon this rock I will build my church; and the gates of Hades will not overpower [or prevail against] it" (v. 18).

THE BRIDE HUNKERS DOWN

Every church today, from manicured megachurch campus to ram-shackle urban storefront, from those bodies that affirm a classically Reformed confession to fellowships that espouse a freewheeling, "Spirit-led" approach—every church today can trace her roots back to Jesus' declaration. The confession itself, those making the confession, and the Christ of that confession are all elements of a church that will be so potent that the gates of hades shall not prevail against it!

And yet . . . when we look at the church today, when we look around at our culture, we wonder. Who's "prevailing" against what? What evidence of transformation in the lives of our people and our communities do we see as a result of the church?

Recently the West paused to pay tribute to the tens of thousands of young men who swarmed ashore at Omaha and Utah and Juno beaches in Normandy, France, more than sixty years ago. From farm and city, from factory and office and classroom, these citizen-soldiers trained and drilled and were equipped with the discipline—and the weapons—to become the most formidable invading force the world had ever seen. It would not be an exaggeration to say that their mission was to save that world from the advancing darkness of Nazism. And to do that, the Allies launched an offensive. They did not hole up on England's south coast under enemy siege.

Neither does the church that Jesus described. He foresaw His church attacking and laying siege to Satan's stronghold, much as an enemy battering ram assaults the gates protecting a city. He promised that He and His church would eventually breach the gates of hell itself.

So why is it that our teaching about the reality of spiritual warfare too often pictures the church hunkered down in a defensive posture rather than an army in full counterattack mode? As long as we accept that image of embattlement, we allow Satan to keep the gates of hades wide open and in full operation in this world!

We don't have to go far to see the signs of those open gates—from same-sex marriages and anti-Christian bias in our schools and universities to the thousands of lives lost to abortion every year and the tolerance of divorce within our own fellowships. But the Enemy's power has not increased; Christ's church has simply failed to take her role seriously. Believers have left the field of battle in droves. Once we sang, with muscular confidence, "Am I a Soldier of the Cross?", "Lead On, O King Eternal," and "Onward Christian Soldiers." Now we shrink from "imposing our values" on others. Live and let live. We have become *precautionary* rather than prevailing.

NO MORE CHURCH IN A BOX

In the last few years I have heard from a growing number of church leaders who are confused by and disillusioned with the proliferation of "church in a box" models that don't transfer to their particular setting and culture, no matter how hard they try. Let me both warn and encourage you: The transformational church is neither a package nor a model. Instead of being a mold, she often breaks molds. The transformational church vision has more to do with the workmanship Jesus Christ wants to accomplish with His church in a specific place—that is, *your* church in *your* community with *your* people. Every transformational church is an original.

Yes, there are common underlying patterns and consistent structural elements in a church that is transformational. I expect that the church you call your spiritual home already exhibits many of these elements. Even more important, however, are *intention* and *direction*—so that a leadership team continually asks: "Are we consciously seeking to be a transforming church?"

So how do you assess your church? Let's go back to Jesus and the Twelve at Caesarea Philippi. Here we find Christ's desires for a intentional, transformational church.

THE TRANSFORMING CHURCH:
LIVING OUT THE CONFESSION THAT CHRIST IS LORD

First, the transforming church is composed of people who live out the confession that Christ is Lord. It should come as no surprise that Jesus continued in the same context and setting of Peter's confession and His own self-revelation by introducing the requirements for being His disciple. In Matthew 16:24–25 (NASB 1977), we read: "Then Jesus said to His disciples, 'If anyone wishes to come after Me, let him deny himself, and take up his cross, and follow Me. For whoever wishes to save his life shall lose it; but whoever loses his life for My sake shall find it.'"

The standards upon which Jesus decided to build His church have never had any room for selective obedience. But you wouldn't arrive at that conclusion looking at many Christians today. A professing follower of Christ is asked if he steals. "Absolutely not." When asked, "Why?" his response is, "I'm a Christian, and God says not to steal." He is then asked, "Have you ever taken someone's life?" Once again, for the same reason he says, "Never." But when asked, as a single thirty-year-old, if he observes sexual abstinence, his response is often a slow and sheepish, "Well, I guess not as much as I should."

Does God's Word equally forbid sexual promiscuity as it does stealing or murder? Absolutely, but today it seems to be in vogue among many Christians to observe a mutated form of Christianity whose central belief turns out to be what I call "selective obedience."

I fully realize that such specific challenges are often met with the concern that Christians must not be legalistic. We are certainly not to select a list of standards we can use to point out the flaws in other Christians' lives. My response to the concern over legalism is to point out that our alternative has almost eliminated our capacity to clearly represent Christ in the world. Whether we look at divorce statistics or other behavioral factors, those who claim to be Christians are looking more and more like the world instead of being salt or light. Yes, Christians fail. But I have far more hope for the effectiveness of a Christian who fails while genuinely trying to be wholeheartedly obedient to Christ than for the Christian who selects a few ways in which he or she will exhibit obedience (and often ends up failing at even those). Christianity with low or no expectations is the Christianity of the precautionary church.

Such thinking was certainly not part of our Lord's prescription for the believers who would constitute the transforming church. He fully and clearly expected His followers to be people who would deny themselves and take up their cross (die to their own desires and pleasures) and follow Him (His example and the teaching of His written Word; see Luke 9:23). That is why Jesus elsewhere (Luke 14:25–35) actually discouraged eager people from becoming disciples until they had seriously counted the cost that would be involved in following Him!

One of the central roles of the church is to be a "safe home" (the other being an effective mission) where the people of God are equipped with an understanding of God's design and plans for our lives. It is in this safe home environment of the church that our people are provided with the following:

- Vital worship that demonstrates the presence and power of God
- True fellowship founded in significant and meaningful relationships
- Biblical instruction and discipleship training grounded in biblical theology
- Pastoral care and shepherding directed toward the needs of the whole person
- Equipping and empowering to do the work of ministry

So the first characteristic of the transformational church is that it is composed of people who are equipped in a safe home to faithfully live out their confession that Christ is Lord, particularly in the areas of obedience that may be under assault at any moment in history. To this first descriptive statement we must add further clarifying statements.

(2) THE TRANSFORMING CHURCH: LIVING OUT THE CONFESSION WITHIN THE SHADOWS OF HADES

Second, the transforming church is composed of people who live out their confession within the shadows of the gates of hades. Jesus lived among people chaffing under Roman occupation. Jesus continually pointed out that His purposes, though falling into the category of warfare, had little or nothing to do with the Roman powers. People expected the Messiah to overthrow the current earthly enemy; Jesus intended to defeat their spiritual foe. The Jews wanted to prevail against Rome; Jesus wanted His followers to prevail against the gates of hades.

In ancient Eastern cultures, the meeting place for the community's authority or ruling body was often at the front gates of the city. Long before city halls, there were city gates. These gates were much more than passages. They represented access, safety, defense, and vulnerability. A fortified city was only as strong as its gates. The term *hades* means literally "not to see." It refers to the unseen, or spiritual world. When Jesus used the phrase "gates of Hades" in Matthew 16:18, He was describing the spiritual stronghold from which Satan and his legions storm out into the world with the assignment and intention of deceiving the lost, destroying the witness of the church, and controlling society.

HOW THE CHURCH SEES HERSELF
AFFECTS HOW SHE ACTS IN THE WORLD

Notice, however, the picture Jesus actually presented in His statement. The gates are a fixed place. They withstand or splinter under the pounding of the battering ram. Jesus was describing a city under assault. He foresaw His church attacking and laying siege to Satan's stronghold. He promised that He and His church would eventually breach the gates of hades. So why is it that our teaching about the reality of spiritual warfare too often pictures the church under siege rather than the church arrayed and battering down the defenses of Satan? Why do we see ourselves in a defensive posture, holding out under attack rather than an army in full counterattack mode?

As long as we accept that precarious, hunkered-down-behind-the-walls description of the church, we allow Satan to keep the gates of hades wide open and in full operation in this world!

Mental imagery makes a difference. How the church sees herself affects how she acts in the world. Perhaps recent events in our country will make military object lessons acceptable once again. They are certainly an integral part of the biblical teaching. My intention in using militaristic language has nothing to do with my desire to glorify the dangers and difficulties of the Christian life and everything to do with my desire to honor and clarify what Jesus told His disciples about His church and her opposition in the world. The same teacher who promised His followers that they would become fishers of men also promised His followers that they would prevail against the gates of hades.

These open gates of hades are blatantly evident within the structures of today's society. It takes only a quick glimpse into the school systems of today to see the evidence of the control and influence of the gates of hades.

Several years ago, a high school student who grew up in our church was suspended from school for merely handing a friend a written announcement of an evening Fellowship of Christian Athletes meeting to be held that night at his home. He passed the note between classes, in a hallway. A watching hall monitor confiscated the note and sent the student to the principal's office. There he received the sentence for his crime—suspension from school.

Without question, the gates of hades are evident today in not only our schools but also in our social clubs, neighborhood gatherings, medical societies, libraries, judicial court systems, and political parties. The gates of hades are regretfully found even amid many modern churches. Satan's power has not increased; Christ's church has simply failed in large numbers to take her role seriously. Believers have left the field of battle in droves. Our view of ourselves as soldiers has become passé or ignored. I wouldn't say the precautionary, hesitant church is losing; I would say this kind of church isn't even seriously trying!

In fact, the gates of hades are prevailing almost unchallenged in the lost world. They must be confronted by believers who will live out their confession within the shadows, laying siege to the gates. The precautionary church is certainly no threat to the unseen authorities; in fact, she has become an aid and ally to them by her silence and lethargy. The hesitant church has a victim mentality, unable or unwilling to take up the offensive. The world is waiting, and the gates of hades are daring the church to be the church!

THE TRANSFORMING CHURCH:
TAKING UP THE BATTLE FOR LOST SOULS

Third, the transforming church accepts its commission to take up the battle for the souls of lost people. To put this characteristic another way, we can say that a transformational church is committed equally to the task of *mission* as it is to the task of *home*. I am using the term *mission* here as a term to describe the church's commitment to reaching the lost, and the term *home* to refer to its task to care for, feed, and protect God's people. (The term *mission* is also used in this book in the sense of ministry plan; see especially chapters 7 and 8.) It is disappointing, to say the least, to see how few churches feel, teach, or carry out a passion for the lost. They may talk "mission," but they don't walk "mission." I am convinced that unless the dual roles of mission and home are equally understood and practiced in the local church we cannot and will not see transformation in our communities.

While on a study leave one summer several years ago, I was evaluating our church and my role as its leader. Throughout those days, I was spending my devotional time in Luke 15, the chapter in which Jesus tells the stories of the lost sheep, the lost coin, and the lost son. During one of my meditation times, I focused on the parable of the lost sheep. Jesus tells how one sheep out of a flock of one hundred goes astray; the shepherd immediately leaves the ninety-nine to search for the one lost.

Keep in mind that sheep feel very insecure when their shepherd is not present and available. In other words, in this story, we have ninety-nine very dissatisfied sheep. Meanwhile, the shepherd, upon finding the one lost sheep, hoists it on his shoulders (v. 5) and comes home rejoicing. Here's Jesus' pointed and profound application of the story: "I tell you that in the same way, there will be more joy in heaven over one sinner who repents than over ninety-nine righteous persons who need no repentance" (v. 7).

Conviction

I am convinced that a majority of the best church members, at least in this nation, do not believe this text. In fact, if you were to disguise this truth and present it without identifying its origin in God's Word, the majority of Christians would reject this teaching as illogical and not representing the values of God.

As I pondered this passage, I wrote the following words in my journal:

> The passion of Christ and His Father is to reach a lost world. For a pastor to embrace this same passion is to make him appear suspect in the best of evangelical churches.

When I share this conviction around the country at pastors' conferences, I find unanimous agreement and identification with this statement. After all, it is "shallow teaching" that reaches the lost, while mature believers need the "deeper truths" that they hire pastors to deliver. And who's for being shallow instead of deep?

In my journal, I continued:

> It's unacceptable to leave the ninety-nine to look for the lost. Church members are very forbearing and forgiving regarding the neglect of the lost; while extremely impatient and unforgiving regarding the neglect of the righteous.

Think of a continuum on which the left end represents an extremely effective "home" function of a church, and the right end represents an extremely effective "mission" function.

After journaling these thoughts, I decided to evaluate the church I pastor in light of this continuum. Believing a healthy and balanced church would find its X placed in the center, I had to honestly admit that our X was placed well left of center—being far more effective as a home to God's people than as a mission to the unchurched.

Lessons from the Flock

Through the years, we have had numerous people leave our church feeling that their needs as believers had not been met, and frankly, many of them had legitimate complaints. Yet what grieves me the most is that never during those years has anyone so much as complained about our ineffectiveness as a mission. Many have left for personal reasons; none have departed because we failed to care for the lost. When have you ever lost a member because your church was failing to effectively reach the lost?

I left my study leave with that convicting evaluation on my heart. I made the commitment to give my best to leading our church in such a way as to find that X placed on the continuum where it needed to be.

That commitment to intentional mission has met its share of challenges. They often come unexpectedly. Here's a good example. I received a phone call from a man out of state whom I had never met. He explained that he was moving his family to Atlanta and that his work would allow him to live anywhere he chose in the city. He had decided to make that decision based on his choice of church. Because time did not allow him to visit churches in Atlanta, he was doing his "church shopping" over the phone. He proceeded to make the following statement and then ask a question. He said, "I have heard that your church is highly committed to reaching the unchurched." He then added, "Don't get me wrong. I am too." Can you guess his next word? You got it! "But," he said, "I need to know if the church's commitment to reach the unchurched could in any way hinder my needs or the needs of my family from being met?"

I was grieved by the mere question. After a lengthy pause, I finally responded by saying, "No, but it is my greatest ambition that one day soon the entire church and its resources will be so given to reaching the unchurched that it could at least be perceived that the believers' needs were being neglected" (though the two are really not at odds with one another, as will be explained later).

The Balance

The truth is that the greatest way to neglect the needs of God's people is to put them in a church that fails to function as a "mission." The healthiest environment for nurture and discipleship is that of "mission." Otherwise, nurture and discipleship become ends rather than means to accomplish God's greater purposes. Unless the twin priorities of "home" and "mission" receive appropriate attention, the church functions without a healthy balance.

I have learned through years of discipling men that I can teach them the truths and commitments of our faith without seeing any automatic by-product of zeal for mission. When I put them in an environment of mission, however, I find them to be hungry and anxious to be fed and nurtured. Much in the way that eating creates no appetite for exercise, so too I have found that Bible study and prayer alone do not create mission-oriented Christians. But, just as exercise creates a desire for food and drink, mission-related activities create an insatiable thirst and hunger to feed on God's Word.

People have asked through the years what accounts for God's great blessing on Perimeter Church. I certainly answer by pointing gratefully to God's grace. Then I add that I often imagine God is in the heavens saying to His angels as they prepare to deliver blessing to many of Christ's local churches around the world, "And keep showering blessings on Perimeter Church. They aren't nearly as effective as they should be, but boy, do they have a passion and commitment to reach the unchurched."

So the transformational church accepts the commission to take on the battle for the souls of lost people. It carries a passion for the lost. It finds ways to reach unreached people. It is supernaturally orchestrated to the end of reaching lost people. And it is greatly disappointed and frustrated until lost people are being won to God's kingdom. Such a church is intentional in carrying out its mission.

The Transforming Church: Winning the Battle Against the Gates of Hades

Fourth, the transforming church wins the battle against the gates of hades. Certainly the ultimate war between God's church and the powers of the unseen world is settled—and the declared victor will be Christ and His church. Jesus has once and forever sealed the defeat of the Evil One by His death and resurrection and has described in His infallible Word the very details of the final battle of this war.

Yet between now and then, God has abundantly provided His church with power to win the daily skirmishes. He has commissioned His church to fight and has promised her power so as to guarantee victory. But the church must be a people who don't compromise their confession and who, walking right into the very shadows of hades' gates, engage the enemy in the battle for the souls of lost people.

Listen: the church will have its struggles and failures. You and I have both seen many of those! But the church has been declared by her Owner and Commander in Chief to be so potent that the gates of hades itself cannot stand up against her. God's church can, should, and ultimately *will* be victorious.

That, in broad strokes, is the picture of a church that is intentional, a church that has power, a church that has influence, a church that transforms souls and communities. If this sounds like the kind of church that God may be calling you to be, then let's get started on this exciting journey.

WHAT MAKES A CHURCH GROW?

*Six Widely Recognized Causes . . .
and a Neglected Seventh Factor*

What causes a church to grow? In one sense, the answer is quite simple. Paul clearly identified the One who causes growth to be God Himself. In fact, he made it clear that "neither the one who plants nor the one who waters is anything, but God who causes the growth" (1 Corinthians 3:7).

In another sense, however, the answer to the question of what makes a church grow can be quite complex. The underlying divine cause may be clear, but the means God uses may vary greatly. We have to admit that skill sets and leadership gifts, facilities and budgets, along with church-growth principles and programs, all contribute to the equation that results in a unique and thriving local church.

The analogy of gardening introduced by Paul in his writing to the church of Corinth (1 Corinthians 3:1–9) is an excellent one for helping us understand church growth. Tim Keller, in an unpublished essay on breaking growth barriers, wrote:

The results of gardening depend on two sets of factors. First, there are the acts of gardening themselves—seeding, watering, weeding, pruning, fertilizing, spraying, etc. Over these factors, the gardener has control. They are a matter of diligence and skill and gift. "I planted the seed, Apollos watered it . . ." (vs. 6). Secondly, there are the contextual factors—the quality of the seed, the weather conditions, and the general conditions of the soil. Over these factors, the gardener has no control. They are matters in God's hands. ". . . but God made it grow . . ." (vs. 7). The power of growth is in the seed. The magnitude of growth is heavily dependent on weather conditions and soil conditions. Yet skillful gardening releases the power of the seed. So we can conclude—if we apply sound gardening principles, there will ordinarily be church growth of quantity and quality. But the amount and magnitude of the growth depends on God's "weather condition" and "soil receptivity"—matters out of your hands. . . . If there is little or no growth, it could be due to weather conditions, but we should first look at the quality of the gardening, so as not to shift blame too quickly!

What factors comprise the quality of the gardening? I suggest seven primary factors are critical for healthy church growth (several of which are factors more or less important depending upon the culture in which the church exists). Six of these are widely accepted, even if they are not very faithfully practiced. The seventh factor describes an overlooked component in church growth. Though often neglected, the seventh factor is crucial to the development of an intentional church.

Let's briefly look at each of the factors.

THE FIRST SIX FACTORS

You might be able to guess at least a few of the first six ingredients essential to an intentional, transforming church. First, of course, is a *biblical theology and polity*. Whether it be a proper understanding of law and grace, the meaning of the gospel as applied to seekers and believers alike, or the relationship between the old and new covenant, a church's theological framework and doctrinal beliefs are critical to its strength and growth. So is a proper understanding of leadership, authority, and organization. A church with weak theology or polity may in fact experience growth, but it may not do so in a healthy way.

Second is *the presence and practice of spiritual disciplines leading to renewal in the body.* "Unless the Lord builds the house, they labor in vain who build it" (Psalm 127:1). Faithful and clear proclamation of God's Word, celebration of the sacraments, vital worship, prayer, Bible study and meditation, and other means to spiritual growth lead to enduring and influential churches.

Third, give to a church *spiritual, discerning, and gifted leadership* who practice what they preach—and watch the congregation follow! Too many churches today are composed of people who are not deep personal worshipers. The leadership of the church needs to set the example here, illustrating how to practice worship, disciple newer believers, and personally lead seekers to Christ.

Fourth, developing a *spiritual and ministry-oriented laity* is essential for a healthy and vibrant church. At times the leadership finds itself complaining about the laypeople. However, it takes time to nurture and develop such servants. With the right encouragement, input, and environment, strong, committed believers will emerge.

Fifth, like it or not, there is a strong connection between church growth and *improved facilities* (including parking). The church I have been privileged to serve for approximately thirty years has occupied five different locations over these years. Each new home had larger buildings and more parking. And, following each move, we experienced significant new growth. The more affluent the area you serve, the higher the expectations for your facilities. But wherever you are, if your space is limited, you forfeit the potential of reaching new people.

Sixth, a growing, transformational church requires *adequate financial resources.* Almost everyone in occupational ministry has heard the statement that when God calls you to ministry, He supplies the financial resources. True as this may be, you and I have both known many ministry leaders chronically handcuffed—and discouraged—because of perennial lack of funds.

Certainly God is faithful. But inadequate education on stewardship, inappropriate and unwise fund-raising techniques, prayerlessness, poor management, and risk-avoidance all play a part in a ministry's financial woes.

Financial resources follow a clearly defined vision. Show me a church with a clearly defined vision as well as both a commitment and a plan to accomplish the vision, and I'll show you a church that most likely will have adequate financial resources.

THE SEVENTH FACTOR

The final factor required for healthy church growth is the most overlooked element when assessing the cause of church stagnation or decline. It is the most complex of the seven factors and requires that leaders address a variety of important subjects. This factor can be best referred to as *an effective ministry plan.*

As important as the first six factors may be, to a great degree they can be neutralized by the failure to have an effective ministry plan. Of course, the first six factors can certainly contribute to the launch of wonderful ministries and explosive churches. But we are targeting a different end and a much longer-term vision. The transforming church is not just a church that grows . . . it is a church that *lasts*! The first six factors will not have a long-term impact without the crucial seventh factor: an effective ministry plan.

A ministry plan consists of a clearly defined purpose, vision, and mission and is supported by a biblically sound and culturally relevant philosophy of ministry. It includes a strategically designed infrastructure and well-documented job descriptions. The overall plan is supported with action plans that define goals, specific action steps, timelines, and resources required to accomplish the vision and mission. Implementation of the plan is measured to determine what's working well and what's not.

To develop an effective ministry plan, the intentional church must address its many functions that rarely align with one another and often seem to operate at far less than peak efficiency. In developing plans that will bring about community transformation, churches need to evaluate two distinctly different sets of functions within church. The first are functions that build up and bring about transformation in the lives of the people within the church. These functions include:

- Leadership development
- Teaching and preaching of God's Word
- Life-on-life discipleship
- Evangelism
- Assimilation of new people
- Caring for God's people

The second are those functions that reach out and bring about transformation within the community through the lives of your people. These functions include:

- Understanding the needs of the community
- Serving the community in its areas of need
- Partnering with other churches and organizations
- Church planting

As you will see, effective ministry plans are developed on the basis of simple processes designed to make mature and equipped followers of Christ and mobilize them for effective transformational outreach in the community.

THE QUEST

For many years, I have taken several weeks in the summer for personal planning, extended prayer, and ministry evaluation. Several years ago during this summer leave, I came to the disappointing realization that what I had dreamed about in church ministry would most likely never come to reality.

My hope of seeing the majority of church members becoming mature and equipped followers of Christ was dimming. From my perspective, the development of such disciples and the process of church as we know it today were quite incompatible. As we reviewed the processes in place for making mature followers of Christ, we knew the expected results were missing. Although we were seeing many good things happen in our church and in our community, integrity demanded a change if we were going to see more of our people becoming mature, equipped followers of Christ.

When I returned home and shared my conclusions with the elders in our church, we had an interesting discussion. They asked if I thought a process existed that could effectively produce mature and equipped disciples. Deep down inside I couldn't help but believe there must be one. But I was uncertain what that process might look like. We had already worked years to build what seemed to be a strong and successful church. Many people were being won to Christ, small-group ministry was thriving, and church growth was constant. Yet we all knew that the potential of the church was far greater than the product.

Our elders commissioned me to take whatever time necessary to discover and return with a plan that could bring the process and product into alignment. I quickly became a diligent student of the process of developing such a ministry plan. We invested a full year of praying and strategizing as we developed a new plan. Having had several years to implement this plan, I am now convinced that the product and process can be married. They are meant to function together. In fact, if the product and the process are estranged in the church, the church will not succeed in fulfilling its vision of becoming a transforming church.

The following chapters detail the different components of an effective ministry plan. Each component will answer a key question about effective ministry. I also will include stories about various aspects from our church's journey of implementing, reviewing, revising and refining key aspects of our ministry plan. My hope is that pastors and church leaders will gain insight from our ministry pilgrimage toward church success and community transformation. But most importantly, I pray for two distinct and balanced results: That your church will not only grow numerically as you produce quality products—mature and equipped followers of Christ—but will also mobilize your people to bring about transformation within your community and other areas you are called to serve. Thus you will truly carry out the mandate of our Lord and Savior, Jesus Christ.

After considering this somewhat different approach to "doing church," I pray you will have new hope for the church. In fact, I believe you will become convinced that we must and can change the way church is done in the next generation. If such changes become reality, to God be the glory.

3

Inside the Effective Ministry Plan
1. A GOD-HONORING PURPOSE

**KEY
QUESTION**
—⁓—
WHY DO
WE EXIST?

Only after I was older and had grown in my knowledge and understanding did I realize that my childhood church did not hold to the authority of God's Word nor promote the true gospel. So it is not surprising that prior to my personal surrender to follow Christ, I wrongly assumed that to live for God's glory would be everything but an enjoyable relationship. I couldn't imagine a less joyous life.

Then I actually met Christ in a personal way. As I grew into my newly birthed love relationship with Him, I was pleasantly surprised to realize that to live for God's glory is to experience the greatest delight a person can know. The very place I suspected held no meaning turned out to be the place that held an inexhaustible supply of glory.

I found my spiritual pilgrimage in an environment rich in historic, biblical theology. Heritage and spiritual roots were honored. Pop theology was discouraged. My early mentors taught me that I didn't need to invent the details of the faith into which I had been spiritually born. I was quickly introduced to the lesson that I was a new participant in a well-established stream of truth that had overwhelming credentials and time-tested answers. Theological giants such as Augustine, Calvin, Owens, Edwards, and Spurgeon were to be read and revered. The Westminster Confession of Faith was put before me as a guide to direct my understanding of Scripture. I was encouraged to memorize the Scriptures and the catechism of the Westminster Divines, which helped me interpret God's Word. As a result of this influence, God became a "big God" to me early on, and for this I am forever thankful.

During those first years of spiritual life, I learned the answer to what is perhaps the most important question a person can ask, "What is man's chief end or purpose in life?" The old catechisms answered this question with great insight into God's design for His creation with the response, "To glorify God and to enjoy Him forever." We should be thankful for theologians such as Jonathan Edwards in the past and John Piper and R. C. Sproul in the present, who have brought such attention and clarity to these words. This answer gives credence to the bigness of God and a worthwhile purpose for us.

WHY DOES THE CHURCH EXIST?

The first step in designing a plan for the church is to determine her purpose. Purpose is determined by answering the question, "Why do we (as a church) exist?"

The purpose of the church is a direct extension of the purpose of man, which therefore leads to the conclusion that "church" is about proclaiming God's glory so that others may enjoy sharing in His renown and splendor. Although it might be stated in somewhat different terms, the chief end or purpose of the church is "to glorify God and to enjoy Him forever."

For a church to exist for any other cause is inexcusable. To exist for helping needy people or benefiting a community, as good as these may appear, is unacceptable to God. Why? Because it elevates a good means and twists it by making it the chief end, or because it replaces an all-embracing, God-centered purpose with a narrow, lesser purpose.

A Lesson from Marriage

This error is similar to (though worse than) a husband who does the right thing for his wife, but for the wrong reason. Picture a husband bringing his wife flowers. Realizing there is no special occasion to celebrate, the wife asks her husband what motivated such a loving action. His answer, "No reason; just to say, 'I love you.'" As she starts to respond with words of appreciation, she is interrupted by her husband. Looking at his watch, he abruptly asks his wife if he can be excused from a commitment he had made to go shopping with her for the day. When she asks, "Why?" his response is, "To allow me to accept an invitation to play golf."

The wife's appreciation immediately turns to fury as she realizes that the flowers are not about "I love you" but rather about "I want to play golf." The very act of giving the flowers becomes repulsive to the wife.

So too are the many reasons for a church to exist that are proposed as substitutes for glorifying God and enjoying Him. The church may be doing the right things, yet for the wrong reasons.

A Friendly Warning

Before we move on and explore other components of developing a ministry plan, I believe that it would be beneficial to offer a word of caution to the highly ambitious pastor. I speak from hard experience as a veteran of guerrilla warfare with the deceitful internal enemy of selfish ambition. Early in ministry I learned that it was easy for me to do the right thing . . . for the wrong reasons. The most dangerous aspect of this warfare is that one can lose the battle against ambition—yet, because ministry success is defined by achievements people can see (such as a packed sanctuary on Sunday), that same ambitious loser can be heralded as a great victor in the world of ministry.

Whether it is the message we preach or the motive by which we serve, we must always address three questions related to ambition. First, is what I am doing or asking other people to do the right thing? Second, is what I am doing or asking others to do being done for the right reason? And third, is what I am doing or asking others to do being done by the right power—the power of the Holy Spirit—not by humanistic self-determination? The object of one's hope in part determines the answer to the second question, which deals with motives.

When one's hope becomes misplaced, wrong motives will certainly follow. I have been reminded, far too often by personal experience, that the object of my hope will dominate my life. If I place my hope in success or man's applause, I will be driven to be successful in man's sight and do what it takes to get that approval. I have learned (am still learning ever so slowly) that improper hope always leads to greater sin—not usually, but always. Any hope other than Jesus eventually leads me out on an ever-thinner limb of sin, which eventually breaks, dropping me into disaster.

WHAT I HOPE IN DETERMINES IN WHOM I HOPE.

I have also learned that what I hope in determines in whom I hope. If I want human success in ministry or to glorify my own reputation, I begin placing my hope in ministry promotion, research, and my own abilities. Yet when my hope is in the work of Christ and His abiding power, I will of necessity put my only hope in Christ.

In the summer of 1990, during a July study leave, I became keenly aware of the devastation brought about by misplaced hope and selfish ambition. I had received word of several fellow pastors who led large, and what seemed to be significant ministries, who had fallen into grievous sin. I wrote in my journal one early morning the following observation and personal caution:

> *Ministries designed to reach the unchurched (thus committed to healthy growth) can easily become vehicles for delivering personal significance through public accomplishment. Large ministries, like large bank accounts, most often become monsters that devour their leaders.*
>
> *Our goal as church leaders should not be to grow large ministries that reach unchurched people but to build discipling ministries that develop mature followers of Christ who, in turn, reach large numbers of unchurched people.*

Though the two approaches to ministry described in my journal may appear to be very similar, the ministry that invests in the individual through discipleship, with the intent of preparing him to reach his lost world, represents an animal much different from the selfish-ambition monster that ultimately devours its leader.

WISDOM

A number of years ago, a small portion of God's wisdom litera-ture began speaking to me quite loudly regarding focus and ambi-tion. The text is found in Proverbs 30:7–9. It reads as follows:

> *Two things I asked of You, do not refuse me before I die: Keep de-ception and lies far from me, give me neither poverty nor riches; feed me with the food that is my portion, that I may not be full and deny You and say, "Who is the Lord?" or that I not be in want and steal, and profane the name of my God.*

I find the author's perception profound. Were I to have only two petitions to make of God and without the insight of this portion of His revelation, I'm sure neither of the author's choices would be mine—and certainly not the part about not giving me riches. Don't get me wrong. A large bank account has never been enticing to me. But riches can be expressed in far more creative ways than simply in terms of money. Would I desire riches in talent, beauty, brains, and opportunity? Emphatically, yes! Would I want my children to have riches in those areas? Once again, yes, without question.

When my first child was born, I was thrilled to have a son. Since I love sports, it was my deep longing that he would be an outstand-ing athlete. Now, I wasn't being greedy. It made no difference to me whether he made it to the NBA, the NFL, or played major league baseball! When my next child, a daughter, was born, I deep down longed for her to be a beautiful child growing into a gorgeous young woman. Later, however, as both of my sons and both of my daugh-ters began to grow up, I noticed that the kids with abundant riches in athletic ability and beauty typically struggled the most in demon-strating good attitudes and humble hearts (qualities, for me, having a much greater premium than abilities and good looks).

The wisdom author's request soon became much more my own, for both my life and for the lives of my kids. Now my prayer was, "Lord, don't give my kids poverty in abilities or beauty lest they struggle with their self-esteem; and don't give them abundant riches in abilities or beauty lest they battle with pride. If I can have my request, Lord, let them be contented and competent, somewhere in the middle."

Please don't take this the wrong way. I'm not advocating a commitment to mediocrity. In fact, God's Word clearly teaches, "Whatever you do, do your work heartily, as for the Lord" (Colossians 3:23). I believe this directive includes everything from the way we groom ourselves to the way we show effort in developing our abilities. Certainly, God determines whether we are rich, poor, or somewhere in the middle. It is not sinful to be rich, nor is it a sign of sinfulness to be poor. We must learn to be content "in whatever circumstances" we find ourselves (Philippians 4:11).

The secret is simply this: If I long to be rich in financial wealth, good looks, athletic ability, or ministry success, and I happen to be given such wealth, I am in the most dangerous of positions. However, if I can believe the wisdom of Proverbs 30:7–9 and know the advantages of having neither poverty nor riches, thus not longing for them, the outcome will be different. Then if God chooses to make me rich, more than likely I will be a good steward of the abundance God has placed in my life. But if I long for riches, and get them, they will probably destroy me.

As a good friend, Fred Smith Jr., once said to me, reflecting on several church leaders who had been ambushed by ambition, "When will the anointing of God be enough?" My prayer for each of us who are naturally ambitious as pastors is that we would see Jesus as our only hope and that our purpose statements would be a constant reminder that we exist "To glorify God and enjoy Him forever."

4

Inside the Effective Ministry Plan

2. A FAITH-ORIENTED COMMITMENT

KEY QUESTION

—⚶—

IS IT THE WILL OF GOD?

The author of Hebrews clearly expressed the importance God places on His followers living by faith: "Without faith it is impossible to please Him" (11:6). Let there be no questions about the importance that "faith living" plays in the life of a church as well as the life of an individual. Ministries that have a mind-set of seeking to follow the leading of God regardless of the likelihood of success are bound to find themselves living within the blessing of God.

When developing a strategic plan for a church, the leadership must first settle this issue: "Will we have a faith commitment or not?" If the answer is yes, then it must ask itself, "In what ways will we demonstrate a faith commitment?" To put it another way, the church's leadership needs to determine early on which question it is going to ask when facing a decision that carries risk. Will it be, "Is it possible?" or "Is it the will of God?" I am convinced the latter is the only appropriate question. Or to put the question in yet another way, "To what degree will we risk failure to bring glory to God?"

About the time I reached the midway mark in seminary, I began earnestly seeking what form my ministry would take upon graduation. Several classmates challenged me to explore the possibility of giving my life to the spiritual needs of people in countries without the opportunities of hearing the gospel so readily available here in the States. It was during this time that the president and founder of Haggai Institute, John Haggai, invited me to join Haggai Institute and to work with Third World leaders advancing the gospel. Though intrigued with this ministry, I sensed that such a call was not the leading of God.

When I met with Dr. Haggai to inform him of my decision, his response dramatically shaped my life and future ministry. His forceful challenge was to "attempt something so great for God that it is doomed to failure unless God be in it."

I couldn't get this challenge out of my mind. It came at the perfect time in my life. Once I adopted this motto, I no longer found myself routinely asking, "Is it possible?" From that point on, the only appropriate question to be considered was, "Is it the will of God?"

SOMETIMES GOD'S WILL INVOLVES OUR FAILURE.

That question has reappeared in some unexpected ways. Early in the life of our church, our handful of first elders was meeting to make some major decisions for our church. One of our elders proposed that we make a bold move and take an unusually large risk (and an expensive one). Upon hearing his recommendation, I responded by saying that though I thought it was a great idea, it didn't appear possible from my perspective. I couldn't have set myself up better for a lesson if I had tried. Now keep in mind I was the one who had been indoctrinating these men with Haggai's challenge, which became our new motto, and stressing the importance of a faith-oriented commitment. I was put in a rightfully humbled position when the same elder responded to me by asking me to quote our often-used motto. No sooner had the words left my lips than he said, "Randy, I would suggest that this recommendation (assuming we have no reason to believe it not to be the will of God) is right on target." We approved the recommendation and found it to be a good decision.

Many people wrongly assume that seeking to do the will of God with proper motives guarantees success. We need to be aware that it is quite possible to do what we think to be God's will and to do so with the proper motive, and still completely fail. Or to put it bluntly, sometimes God's will involves our failure.

When seeking to make our first church property purchase, we found a piece of property that seemed to have our name written all over it. However, the price of the property was well beyond the reach of the $40,000 land fund we had worked so hard to raise.

Unsolicited by me or anyone else, a group of out-of-town business leaders who knew of our need for property and were friends of our church made us a gracious offer. They were willing to invest in a limited partnership to purchase the property on our behalf. It would be our responsibility to get the limited partnership sanctioned by the Securities and Exchange Commission and then to make offerings to groups in various cities that these friends of our church would arrange for us to meet. But there was indeed a risk.

The earnest money required to hold the property while awaiting approval from the Securities and Exchange Commission was $40,000 (our total land fund). Both business and spiritual counsel unanimously encouraged us to take the risk. We prayed and we waited for government approval to allow us to raise the money. Though the prospectus was eventually approved, the clearance came only a few days before the expiration date of our contract. Without enough time to go to enough cities to make our offering, our time expired and the property was awarded to a backup contract that was submitted after ours. Not only did we lose the property, we lost our earnest money (our entire land fund).

Immediately, monies began to be given to us from some of these same friends as well as unusually generous giving from our people (who would rather have failed attempting something great than never risking failure and accomplishing little or nothing). Within a few months, our bank account was larger than what we originally had. We ended up getting a piece of property that never seemed as ideal as the first piece.

For years, I regularly drove by that original piece of property, which now housed a massive apartment complex. Seeing the size still to be four times the size of our then present property and on a major road with high exposure, I often wondered why God had allowed us to fail in our endeavor. Years passed before He allowed me to get a small glimpse into His "higher ways."

Approximately eight years later, we came to the realization that our original purchased property, even with an additional ten acres purchased, was not sufficient to serve our growing church. In the providence of God, He provided a piece of property two and a half times larger than the piece we had lost and in a much more suitable location. I am convinced we would never have made such a move had we built on the original property.

And in an eye-opening postscript, our original site recently became ground zero of a massive tornado that ripped the apartment complex off its foundation and essentially demolished it. Had we gotten our own way, our church would have been destroyed.

Certainly, when we attempt something we have every reason to believe is honoring to God, and even if we have the right motives, it is still possible to fail. Yet when there is failure, we can know that ultimately we will be better off because of the failure.

RELOCATION

Leading a church with a faith-oriented commitment can be a painful experience. It often reveals the fear produced by the weakness of one's faith. Certainly, I am no exception. The following story illustrates this well.

Earlier, I alluded to our church's undertaking a relocation. At the time, our church was approximately twelve years old. Our leadership unanimously agreed upon this decision. Embracing our well-worn motto, we asked what we thought God's will was regarding the amount of property. Using a formula we felt appropriate to give us that answer, we were astounded to discover that we would need seventy-five acres at a minimum. Though "doomed to failure unless God be in it," we began the preliminary steps toward relocation.

We established a maximum budget we thought generous but appropriate, and hired two commercial Realtors (members of our church) to search for suitable sites. Based on the criteria given them, only one property, a hundred-acre piece, met every specification on the list. However, the asking price of the property was several times more than our allotted budget, and the property was already under contract for purchase. The owner dismissed our offer and our real estate agents continued their search.

After making no progress in locating another suitable site, I asked our two agents to go to the owner and present our offer once again.

They returned to say that the owner had no interest in our offer and that the property was still under contract. Yet again, after weeks of a failed attempt to find another appropriate piece of property, I asked these same two men to do me a personal favor and revisit the owner one last time. Though unenthusiastic, they agreed to go. To their amazement, they found that the owner had lost his previous contract and needed to sell the property quickly. He accepted our original offer without negotiation.

Potential Snag

During our period of due diligence before closing on the purchase, I was walking the property. A neighbor who lived adjacent to it, curious as to my presence, asked me who I was. When I told her, she congratulated us for putting the property under contract but quickly told me that we would never get the use permit required to use it for a church. I asked what made her think that. She explained that another neighbor whose property was also adjacent to our property was the president of the largest and most powerful homeowners association in North Atlanta.

This homeowners president would fight us and would definitely win, she assured me. I promptly got the president's name, gave it to our relocation director, and urged him to become the president's close friend—and very quickly! Yet, before he could initiate contact, she called him and invited him to attend their upcoming homeowners association meeting. He asked why, and her response was, "To see how enthusiastically I'm going to support your request for a church use permit." He was obviously surprised and curious.

He candidly told the president what he had heard regarding her probability of fighting our usage request. She explained that seven years previously she had become a Christian and had been given the gift of faith and a ministry of prayer. She explained that during these seven years, this large tract of land behind her home had been her prayer garden. For seven years she had prayed that God would keep that property for someone who would use it for His glory.

"We've opposed one potential purchaser after another and won each time," she added, "but when I heard it was Perimeter Church who was buying the property and knew of your reputation in the community, I knew it was God's will for me to enthusiastically support your usage of the property." Our request was subsequently approved unanimously.

Lesson on the Court

Now with such a supernaturally orchestrated event, one would think that we would demonstrate great faith throughout the relocation project. However, this was not the case. Our attempts to raise the money necessary to pay for the property, sell our existing facilities, and raise the money for a new facility all seemed to flounder. The outlook turned bleak. As summer arrived, I left for my annual two-week study leave. I told my wife, Carol, that I sensed God was perhaps leading me to leave Perimeter and search for another ministry. She was shocked, and I found myself grieved over the sense of leading I was feeling. I have never before or since had such a sense.

During my last week of study, I stayed in a friend's home in another city. This friend had been a professional tennis teacher for years and had helped teach me to play. Throughout the years I had never beaten him in a match. The day before I was to leave to return to Atlanta, he and I played. I beat him for the first time ever. He was as shocked as I was and immediately challenged me to a match the following morning before I left for home. In his words, "I want to see if this was really a fluke." I didn't want to play, desiring to leave town with a final win under my belt. But I couldn't avoid the match. I believe he beat me "love and love"—shutting me out both sets.

> AS MUCH AS I FEAR FAILURE, I HAVE GROWN TO FEAR THE ABSENCE OF RISK IN A FAITH COMMITMENT EVEN MORE.

Following the match, he commented that though he had seen me play poorly in the past, he had never seen me not try to win. He asked what was wrong. I had to admit to him that I had not tried and that my reason was nothing short of a fear of failure. I knew if I didn't try, I could easily excuse my loss.

God used this episode as a picture to reveal to me that the same was true in regard to our relocation. I wasn't sensing Him leading me to leave Perimeter. I was merely afraid of failure, just as in the tennis match. I had become convinced that we were not going to accomplish the relocation and personal humiliation would be the result.

One morning after I returned home, I was reading Exodus regarding the journey of the Israelites under Moses' leadership. I was prompted to write the following in my journal.

I've led our church to the seashore. There's no way out, and Pharaoh's army is getting closer and closer. I'm sure the troops are beginning to wonder whether the water is going to part. My confidence in my ability to get the people across the sea has vanished—and that's good—but in light of the diminished confidence I have found myself both frightened and discouraged. Part of my fear is my growing concern that the closer Pharaoh gets, the more unwilling our congregation might be to stand in faith to see the waters part. But I am committed to leading them across those waters—not all will go with us, but win or lose, we're going to finish the race!

As much as I fear failure, I have grown to fear the absence of risk in a faith commitment even more. Now I long to observe the benefits received from being part of a church that demonstrates a faith-oriented commitment to the purpose of glorifying God—such as watching old paradigms of ministry be broken in the formation of new ones, and most important, receiving the blessing of watching God, time and time again, do what some (including me) thought was impossible. Once again, let me illustrate.

BEGINNINGS

After arriving in Atlanta to plant Perimeter Church, we began trying to assemble a core group committed to working with us in raising up this new church. Within a couple of months, God gave us five families to colabor with us in this endeavor. We decided that we needed to secure a place to worship on Sunday mornings. We agreed to set a prayer target, specifically asking God to give us our needed meeting place by a certain date. We all agreed to pray for a secured facility by that date and to participate in locating such a facility.

One person was assigned to look at schools, another to contact real estate agents, another to check out hotels, office areas, and similar matters. On the date we had set as a prayer target, we all reported no success in finding an appropriate facility. Early that afternoon, I sat in my home office disappointed that God seemed not to have answered our prayer.

As I sat there, the name of Cecil Day came to my mind. He was the founder and president of Days Inns of America. Though I had never met him, I had heard wonderful things of his Christian faith wherever I had been in Atlanta. Perhaps only because of a formerly declared faith-oriented commitment, I decided to make a cold call on Mr. Day, not even knowing if he was in town, much less in his office with time to meet with me. As I was leaving, Carol, my wife, asked where I was going. I told her "to meet with the founder of Days Inn." She was impressed until she found out I didn't have an appointment. When she questioned why I wouldn't call first, my response was that he certainly wouldn't let me see him without an appointment and today was the date for which we had prayed.

Upon arriving at his office, I found his secretary had stepped out of the reception area. Seeing his name on the door behind her desk, I decided to risk it. I opened the door cautiously, only to find Mr. Day leaving his office. I quickly introduced myself to him and explained what I was seeking. I told him I was not asking for a gift but only a facility to rent. He graciously heard me out and sent one of his employees with me to look at the old Day Realty Company headquarters that had just been vacated.

Though it was small and well-worn, it looked like a royal palace to me. I expressed interest in leasing the property and asked what the rental price was. The man told me that Mr. Day was going to give it to us (because it was for a church) at half the asking price. That price came out to $1,700 a month! I nearly fell over in shock. We had no offerings and no savings yet.

Mr. Day's representative then informed me of an additional utility cost of $300 a month. Two thousand dollars a month might as well have been $2 million. Before I could decline the gracious offer, the employee told me that Mr. Day had told him to let him know if I was interested in leasing the space. In his words, "Mr. Day said he may want to give you an additional discount."

I told him once more we were definitely interested. I figured Mr. Day might offer an additional 10 percent discount. But it didn't take me long to tally the discount. I was a math major in college, and I could easily figure out 10 percent of $2000—and the difference was meaningless. Yet before I could say anything, the employee had called Mr. Day to tell him of our interest.

The man's mouth fell open when he hung up. He looked at me and said, "Mr. Day is giving you quite a discount. He said the price for you will be $50 a month and no utilities." (I tried to get him down to $25! Not really.) Once again, God had honored a faith-oriented commitment.

"DARE MIGHTY THINGS"

The benefits of a faith-oriented commitment are many. Whether the advantage of determining the decision-making process, or allowing us to see God do what was seemingly impossible, none, however, compare to the satisfaction experienced from knowing that God was honored and thus pleased.

In 1899, Theodore Roosevelt said, "Far better to dare mighty things, to win glorious triumphs, even though checkered by failure, than to take rank with those poor spirits who neither enjoy much nor suffer much, because they live in the gray twilight that knows not victory nor defeat." Though in full agreement, I would go further. I would say, "Far better to attempt something great for God and fail, and yet still hear Him say in eternity, 'Well done, good and faithful servant; you have pleased Me by your life of faith,' than to succeed in great things yet fail to hear His applause because of our lack of faith."

Success or failure in what is attempted is not the central issue. It is honoring God with a faith-oriented commitment and living out the belief that we live under the control and with the indwelling power of the King of Kings. When a church exists for the single purpose of glorifying God and enjoying Him and operates with a faith-oriented commitment—watch out! There you will find the makings of a transforming church.

Early in your strategic ministry planning, embrace a faith-oriented commitment married to a God-honoring purpose, and then get ready to enjoy the blessings of a church that pleases God.

5

Inside the Effective Ministry Plan
3. A GOD-GIVEN VISION

KEY QUESTION

WHAT ARE WE
SEEKING TO
ACCOMPLISH?

If the purpose of the church answers the question, "Why do we exist?" the vision of the church is established by answering the question, "What are we seeking to accomplish?" Likewise, if a faith-oriented commitment prepares us to take risks, a God-given vision holds us accountable to take the right risks.

The next step in developing a strategic ministry plan involves defining what God is calling the church to accomplish, that is, knowing God's vision for your church. Until the church's leadership reaches agreement on this vision, the church cannot move forward.

THE POWER OF VISION

In May 1961, in one of the most famous speeches of his presidency, John F. Kennedy presented a vision to our nation and to our space program that stretched our thinking and challenged our ability to achieve: "I believe that this nation should commit itself to achieving the goal, before this decade is out, of landing a man on the moon and returning him safely to the earth." In communicating this vision, he clearly acknowledged the enormity of the goal when he said: "No single space project in this period will be more impressive to mankind, or more important for the long-range exploration of space; and none will be so difficult or expensive to accomplish."

A VISION GAINS CREDIBILITY WHEN IT CLEARLY RESTATES AND APPLIES BIBLICAL TRUTH.

While Kennedy's vision may have seemed impossible to the majority of people in 1961, his vision for the nation was accomplished on July 20, 1969, when Neil Armstrong took mankind's first step on the moon and made his historic statement, "That's one small step for man, one giant leap for mankind."

A clear focused vision defining a tangible long-term goal motivates people to accomplish things that they would otherwise think impossible. In 1 Chronicles 28, King David shared the vision and plans for building a temple for God. First Chronicles 29 reports that the people responded with joy and gave willingly to provide the resources necessary to make the vision and plans for the temple a reality.

A BIBLICAL FOUNDATION

In Matthew 28, Christ gave a vision to His disciples that has been handed down to us through the ages, "Therefore go and make disciples of all nations, baptizing them in the name of the Father and of the Son and of the Holy Spirit and teaching them to obey everything I have commanded you" (vv. 18–20 NIV). The Great Commission actually gives us two components of vision to consider.

First, the Great Commission gives us a vision for the *transformation* that we are to bring about *in* the lives of each person. Specifically, the church is called to make disciples who are trained to obey and put into practice the teaching of Christ and His Word. As a new believer is equipped and matures, Christ tells us in John 15 to expect that we will see fruit in the life of the believer who is to be mobilized and directed into the community.

Second, the Great Commission gives the church the vision of the *transformation* it is to bring about *through* the lives of its people—make disciples of all nations. Acts 1:8 provides additional perspective on the church's role in fulfilling the vision to reach and transform the world, "You shall be My witnesses both in Jerusalem, and in all Judea and Samaria, and even to the remotest part of the earth."

One way of thinking about these geographical locations is to consider Jerusalem as representing those people who are both *geographically and relationally close* to your church. Judea and Samaria represent those who are *geographically close but relationally distant*. The remotest part of the earth represents those who are *both geographically and relationally distant* from the church. While the role of witness will vary with each location, it is clear from the Scripture that this is to be a part of the vision of a transformational church.

IS YOUR CHURCH PURSUING A CLEARLY DEFINED VISION?

What's your vision for your church? Have you thought about it? Have you defined it? Have you articulated it to your leadership team, staff, and key lay leaders?

Intentional churches are driven by a vision. Simply stated, vision answers the question, "What are we trying to accomplish?" The process of developing a vision statement involves seeking God, listing elements to be encompassed by the statement, seeking input and affirmation from elders, and then distilling this work into a short, memorable statement that defines what the church is trying to accomplish. The following are characteristics of an effective vision statement for a church seeking to become a transformational church:

- It must be based on a faith-oriented commitment that reflects a God-sized, "unless God be in it" goal.
- It defines the transformation the church is working to accomplish *in* the lives of its people; that is, to fulfill the Great Commission command to make disciples.
- It defines the *transformation* the church is working to accomplish *through* the lives of its people; that is, it establishes the scope and breadth of the church's intended reach and transformational impact.

WHO RECEIVES THE VISION?

This creates an interesting discussion about whose responsibility it is to receive the vision from God. Certainly, the polities of various churches differ from one another. Although churches have differing procedures in place to discern their God-given vision, it appears that God usually gives vision for ministry to individual leaders, at least at the initial step. In our church's experience, the clarifying of the vision often comes as members of the leadership team raise concerns or ask probing questions. Although the pastor must accept a significant responsibility for receiving the vision, he should never take this role in an autonomous way. I have found that the elders in our church have had a powerful ministry in my life by schooling my mind. Their combined wisdom has repeatedly helped me see and understand aspects of God's work that I missed because of my limitations. In fact, I have discovered that a significant aspect of God's rule in my heart involves my willingness to hear Him speak through the wisdom of other godly leaders.

I offer the following advice to leadership boards who are seeking to determine what God has for their churches' visions: *Send your pastor on the quest for such a picture. Make taking time to listen to God a priority in your pastor's job description.*

DECISION MAKING

Early on in the life of our ministry, I assumed it best to invite our elders to escort me through any attempt to evaluate our vision. Together we would consider whether God was directing us to a new view of His plans for us or if He was simply reaffirming our present vision. Because I normally lead through the means of gaining consensus, I asked the elders to work as a team to seek God's leading.

Much time was spent in personal thought and prayer. As time passed I became more and more convinced of God's leading but continued my monthly dialogue with our elders. Though we ultimately arrived at the same conclusion, I sensed more had been lost than gained in the process. Though we gained consensus, we experienced numerous bumpy roads en route and certainly spent more time debating the issues than seemed wise from the perspective of time stewardship.

After all was said and done, I called church consultant and author Lyle Shaller, whose wisdom I greatly respect, and asked him to evaluate the process we had just completed. His evaluation was profound. He suggested that when we do this in the future, recognize that God would probably initially lead most clearly through me. He described the ideal process as follows.

The senior pastor has the responsibility to take the lead in the development of the vision statement, Shaller advised. He recommended that I should have "gone to the mountain to seek the voice of God." After believing I had heard His voice, I should then have gone back to our elders, who in our system of polity function as my authority. He recommended that if the elders could not, at that point, affirm my sense of God's leading, then I should go once again to the mountain, spending time listening to God. Whether I sensed that God led in the same way I had perceived on my first trip or sensed that God led in a different direction, I should share that with our elders. If, again, they could not embrace this new vision, then perhaps yet another such mountain visit and subsequent reporting should take place. If, however, after three times we could not agree, Lyle suggested that I should then resign. If the elder team and I could not agree on vision, then I, as the subordinate in our polity, should seek another opportunity of service where my vision and my leadership team's direction could be in harmony.

This approach allows a shared leadership structure to function at its best. It places the responsibility of receiving the vision on one person but maintains the significant role of confirming that vision within a group of fellow leaders. It assigns important initiating authority to a leader without creating an autocratic condition where the vision of the leader is imposed on others just because he believes it is God-given. Sometimes a difference in vision requires parting of the ways (note the separation of Paul and Barnabas in Acts 15:36–41).

HOW DOES VISION COME?

Perhaps the most often asked question regarding vision is, "How do you receive it?" Even as churches differ in the polity, they also differ in their theology. My intention at this point is not to defend my particular theology but rather to share from a personal perspective what I have learned and experienced about receiving a vision.

First of all, the word *vision* denotes many different things to different people. Some think immediately of a mystical trance or perhaps a particular sign gift. Some would assume an audible voice experience, whereas others would immediately think of a revelation from God, perhaps in the likeness of one received by the apostle Paul. My sense of gaining a vision from God is much less dramatic but no less dynamic. Let me describe how I go about seeking vision from God by describing the manner I went about gaining our original vision for Perimeter Church.

After Dr. Haggai had challenged me to a faith-oriented ministry, I began logging hour after hour alone with God seated with pencil and paper. Knowing that He alone could reveal to me that to which He would call me, I began each private session asking God to give me ideas as to what He would have us accomplish. Specifically, I was seeking elements of a vision we could wholeheartedly pursue and know that it would honor Him if it succeeded, but be doomed to failure unless He were in it.

Now I realized that every thought that came to mind had no guarantee of being a thought from God. Yet having cleansed my heart and invited His presence, I was certain that among the many ideas recorded, certain ones might perhaps be prompted by Him—some of which could well be the very vision elements to which God would call me to give my life.

I am sure I spent nearly a hundred hours alone with God immersed in this communication experience. I kept a clipboard during this particular spiritual discipline and recorded page after page of ideas. I wrote down every thought I perceived as potentially given by God or at least worthy of further consideration. I reviewed them periodically. I asked counsel from those who knew me best regarding many of the ideas but relied mainly on asking God to burn deep within my heart those thoughts that were given by Him. Though I never expected to hear an audible voice, my goal was that certain ideas conceived while alone with God would burn so deeply into my heart and mind that they would be as certain to me as if I had audibly heard from God.

It was during this time that I sensed with great confidence that God was calling me to plant a church unlike any I had experienced. The church in my mind's eye would seek such accomplishments that they would be doomed to failure unless God was in it. I was absolutely convinced that if my vision were merely humanly attainable even with great effort, it would not be a God-given vision. The more this vision took hold in my life, the more I realized I would rather fail miserably pursuing it than succeed at a lesser ideal.

I knew that to avoid opposition from traditional thought I would need to be the first person involved, which led me to believe planting a church from scratch would be wise. God used several events to make me believe Atlanta was the community in which to plant the church. As time passed, the clipboard pages continued to accumulate. Several months after beginning the quest, I had a picture in my mind, and described on paper, of a church that I find amazingly similar to the actual church that has evolved over these years.

Adventure in Atlanta

I am always disappointed to hear soon-to-be church planters describe their future church as a "such and such" type of church—referring to a church patterned exactly like a dynamic, well-known church in some other community. The reason for my disappointment in part is that they are forfeiting the possibility of being part of a signature ministry designed uniquely to fit a one-of-a-kind leader and community. But even beyond this, I am jealous for the church planter to experience that sense of profound leading from God that so greatly enhances one's own faith-oriented commitment.

For instance, when my wife, Carol, and I eventually moved to Atlanta, I had just graduated from seminary. Our first child was less than two months old. The Presbyterian Church in America had hired me to plant a church in Atlanta. They had done so reluctantly. It had been their policy not to begin churches without an established core group, but because I came with my clipboard in hand and the sense of calling so intense to plant from scratch, they were willing to sidestep policy and to approve my request. They had sent us to secure an apartment in Atlanta prior to my graduation and had agreed to pay us $1,200 a month for up to twelve months, as needed. So all was set.

However, I had not considered the fact that my income flow would cease between the time I left graduate school and the end of the first month after arriving on-site to begin church planting. We had no plan for our finances during this time, but we did have a sense of calling so strong that we knew (certainly not infallibly) we were to go ahead and move to Atlanta. By the time we actually arrived, all we had left was ten dollars, an apartment without utilities, an empty refrigerator, and an obligation to pay our first month's rent.

Up to the very day we had arrived in Atlanta, we had remained confident that God would supply our every need. But as Friday afternoon ticked away (the designated time for me to pay our rent), all such confidence evaporated. I felt obligated to explain our situation to the apartment manager. Carol and I anxiously wondered what her response would be. As I entered the office, after delaying as long as possible, I said to the manager, "I guess you need our money now?" The manager looked at me with a look of apology and responded by saying, "I am so sorry. I forgot about your payment and have already taken our money to the bank today. I am not allowed to leave money in the office over the weekend." Then the manager continued by asking me, "Would it be OK with you if you paid us first thing Monday morning?"

I looked at the manager with a disguised sense of relief and answered, "Sure, if that helps you, waiting will be fine with me." I hurried home with renewed hope, calculating what we needed God to supply during our unexpected reprieve. Our minimum budget for the remaining weeks until my first paycheck, including apartment rent, was approximately $600. Now, two extra days renewed my confidence of God's coming provision.

I AWOKE, GOT ON MY KNEES, AND CRIED OUT TO GOD IN CONFUSION AND UNBELIEF.

As I entered the apartment, I could see Carol was anxiously awaiting the outcome. I excitedly told her, "Carol, you know God always waits until the last moment to provide His people's needs so as to build their faith. The last moment is not till Monday morning. You watch," I announced to her in somewhat prophetic tones, "God will supply our money through the Saturday mail." I was convinced this was how it would happen for three reasons. One, we had left our new address with many friends who were aware of our excursion to Atlanta. Second, we did not know anyone in Atlanta who could possibly be used to supply our need. And last, I had heard of many Christian leaders receiving exact amounts of financial needs through the mail. I assumed it would happen that way for us as well.

The following morning we found ourselves in the mid-June heat and humidity of Atlanta in an apartment without utilities—awaiting the arrival of the mailman. We anxiously and hopefully kept a lookout until the mailman arrived and passed us by without delivering a single letter. At that very moment my heart sank and my feeble hopes vanished. I began to seriously doubt that God would provide our need. In fact, during that night I was so burdened with the responsibility of a newborn and no means of provision that I awoke, got on my knees, and cried out to God in confusion and unbelief.

I knew God was not obligated to provide for us the way in which I felt He would or should. I knew that our move to Atlanta was not revealed in Scripture (the only will of God we can know to be infallible). Yet my sense of having received a vision and call from God was so clear that the events of the moment made no sense. I was honest with God and told Him that I felt abandoned in a mission to honor Him.

The next morning was Sunday. Here we were, in Atlanta as a pastor and family, without a church. We decided to attend perhaps the largest church in Atlanta at that time, First Baptist. We parked and were approaching the front steps of the church when we met an old college friend of mine leaving the earlier service. This friend was one in whose life God, by His grace, had used me while in school. Later, on a couple of occasions, he had sent me a financial gift during my seminary years. Both times I had returned the money, urging him to give it to someone in greater need. Immediately, I remembered that money, knowing he would be more than happy to help us now in our time of financial need. (After all, that was my money I had sent back to him!)

After we greeted each other warmly, he asked me what I was doing in Atlanta. I explained we were here to plant a new church. He was intrigued and suggested that we sit on the back pew and catch up during the early part of the service. He said that he would leave before the sermon, having already attended the earlier service. As we were walking into the church, I was already thanking God for His provision. However, before we could be seated, I had a sense that God was speaking to me. Once again, no audible voice, but a sense of conviction in my conscience that was so strong, I might as well have heard an audible voice. I knew God was telling me not to mention our financial need. Not that it would have been wrong for someone else in the same situation or even for me in a similar but different situation. But I knew that God was prompting silence.

Begrudgingly I submitted and remained quiet. Nothing was ever mentioned about financial needs. As the offering plates were being passed, I noticed that my friend was filling out a check. I thought nothing of it, assuming he was preparing his gift perhaps missed in the earlier service. I passed the plate to him. He handed the plate to the usher without adding his check to the offering. He immediately turned to me, stuck the check inside my shirt pocket, and said, "I hope you'll accept this. I've wanted to do something for you for a long time." I immediately said, "I will!" No return of this money! The only question left unanswered, thundering in my mind was, "Did he give us enough money?" It would have been inappropriate to ask how much he had given me, so I just thanked him and anxiously awaited the beginning of the sermon so that my friend would leave and I could check out the amount of the gift.

To my great disappointment, my benefactor did not leave when the sermon began but rather chose to sit through the entire service. That was unquestionably the longest sermon I have ever sat through! I would watch when he turned his head and I would quickly glance into my pocket to see if the amount was in sight—never success-fully. Finally, the service ended and my friend left. I quickly pulled out the check to find it to be $600—just what we needed. Some might call that coincidence—but not me! In fact, I'm convinced God in-tervened in time and space and divinely provided us with that gift. And He did it in a unique and memorable way.

The point is that were it not for a strong sense of a God-given vision, we would probably have never been so eager to launch out with enough faith-oriented commitment to have been sitting there on Sunday morning. We watched God continue to bring to reality that which would have otherwise seemed doomed to failure.

DEVELOPING THE VISION AT PERIMETER

Earlier I reported spending perhaps a hundred hours alone with God seeking a vision given by Him. When all was said and done, numerous conceptual components became ingredients of that vision. Since we call this entity a "vision," let me describe what I saw in my mind's eye. This was the profile of the church I felt called to plant:

First, I saw a church that could impact an entire metropolitan city by the quality of its disciples. Second, I saw a church geograph-ically broad enough to touch people throughout the entire city. Third, I saw a church sociologically, economically, and culturally diverse enough to reach every kind of people in Atlanta. Last, I saw individual congregations of equipped believers linked together to alter the spiritual, political, educational, and social structures of Atlanta—that is, a church that would bring Atlanta into an encounter with the kingdom of God.

I cautiously concluded that this vision was God-given, but I realized that only time would tell. Without question, the effort would be faith-oriented for two reasons. First, I had no idea how to design such a church, nor had I ever seen or read of a church with a similar vision. Second, and more significant, was the reality that with me as this church's pastor, such a vision was certainly "doomed to failure unless God be in it."

THE FINAL, WRITTEN VISION

The point has been made that a vision is useless until it is written. Perhaps this is a bit of an overstatement. Yet it is typically the case that if you can't write down the vision, then you probably cannot articulate it well enough to cast it for those who are capable of making it a reality. As mentioned previously, a well-written vision, simple and brief, is a God-sized idea expressed in a way that can be understood, remembered, and repeated to others.

Scripture has an important role in the writing of a church vision. A vision gains credibility when it clearly restates and applies biblical truth. Conversely, a vision that violates biblical principles may be vivid, exciting, and even bold, but it will not be God-given.

Although Perimeter's vision expresses our immediate concern with our neighboring community, "where we serve" represents the threefold breakdown of geographical scope found in Acts 1:8 discussed at the beginning of this chapter. Perimeter's written vision answers the question, "What are we trying to accomplish?" in the following way:

We are seeking to bring the people of greater Atlanta and all places where we serve into a life-transforming encounter with the kingdom of God.

Here are the characteristics of such a life-transforming encounter within a community:

- its people, in ever increasing numbers across ethnic and socioeconomic boundaries, are becoming members of Christ's body, the Church, becoming passionately committed to Him engaging in Word and Deed ministry;
- its believers' lifestyles are becoming increasingly marked by high moral standards, practicing indiscriminate love, demonstrating spiritual integrity in all their relationships, living by faith in Christ attempting faith-oriented goals, and speaking the truth regardless of the consequences;
- its churches increasingly work together in the unity of the Spirit, as the body of Christ, ministering to the needs of the community, working for justice for the powerless and for reconciliation;
- its educational, judicial, political, business, and social structures increasingly begin to reflect being in conformity with the Word of God.

Every new member of Perimeter Church is introduced to this vision. We take a significant amount of time to explain the background of each point and allow questions for clarification. Every elder, deacon, and discipleship leader is required to memorize it and embrace it. I can't emphasize enough how important it is that your church's vision be God-given, well articulated in writing, and cast before your people as often and in as many forums as possible. Such a vision is a foundational block in building a transformational church.

6

Inside the Effective Ministry Plan

4. WELL-PRIORITIZED VALUES

KEY QUESTION

WHAT IS MOST IMPORTANT TO US?

W hat belief, activity, or custom, if forbidden in your church's life, would make its ministry not worth continuing? Or, to put it in different terms: What is most important to your church? Better yet: What is absolutely indispensable?

When you have clearly answered these questions, you have just described your church's values.

STATED AND UNSTATED VALUES

Many, if not most, churches have a set of *written* values (things desired or expected to be most important) and a set of *unstated* values (to which the church faithfully adheres every day). Visitors and new members know about the stated values. The unstated values are shared and honored by the insiders. The formal, written values are relatively easy to change. The unstated values seem to be carved in invisible stone.

An intentional church should know and state its values. A church that desires to effectively transform its people and community identifies and honestly evaluates its hidden values because they affect every aspect of church life. And if you think identifying and evaluating those unstated values is difficult, wait until you witness an institution such as a church endeavoring to actually alter its unstated values. But the truth is that unless a church is willing to put its unstated values on the table for examination, any talk about change will be fruitless. More on this later in the chapter.

"WHO WE ARE" AND "WHAT WE DO"

One of our most challenging exercises in developing a ministry plan was to agree on a short list of appropriate values. During an annual officers' retreat (which involved about one hundred elders and deacons), I asked our leaders to gather in groups of ten and make a list of five core values that defined our church. Out of the approximately ten sets of five values, there was amazingly little duplication. Some thought in terms of "who we are" values, such as love or integrity. Others identified "what we do" values, such as outreach or discipleship. Still others listed what I call "how we do ministry" values, such as small groups or cultural relevance.

ONE OF A LEADER'S KEY RESPONSIBILITIES IS TO KNOW AND TO HOLD HIMSELF AND OTHERS ACCOUNTABLE TO THE PRIORITY OF VALUES.

These different perspectives provided plenty of content for a lengthy discussion. We finally arrived at a short list in each of these three categories and developed a description of our beliefs regarding each. Then we asked ourselves an important prioritizing question: "Which of these sets of values are most important to us?"

Without question, the list of four values that describes "who we are" as a church won out. Those values included love, integrity, faith, and truth (remembered by the acrostic LIFT). If we don't demonstrate love, hold to integrity, exhibit faith, and embrace the truth, then we should not exist as a church.

The second set of values important to us is our "what we do" values. We have determined that of all the things the church is called to do we will set three priorities as most important to us. These are our "what we do" values:

1. We glorify our God through public and private worship.
2. We grow in our faith by fellowship and equipping.
3. We give ourselves away in service, mercy, evangelism, and stewardship.

The last of our three sets of the values are the "how we do ministry" values. For us these include every-member ministry, equipping, cultural relevance, and small groups. Although we educate our leadership about this third set of values, our people at large rarely hear us talk about them. Two sets of values are as much as they can digest and certainly all they can remember.

CHANGING EXISTING VALUES

Once the formal and the unstated values are out in the open, the real work begins. The most difficult ideals to change are the "who we are" values. The "what we do" and "how we do ministry" values will usually fall in line if the "who we are" values are clearly understood and then preserved.

The character of the church's leadership, in essence, determines such values. One of a leader's key responsibilities is to know and to hold himself and others accountable to the priority of values. Sometimes, the only way to change (or preserve) values involves a change of leadership. An existing or potential leader who cannot subscribe wholeheartedly to the core values of the church forfeits his or her leadership role.

Once the church's "who we are" values have been stated and prioritized, they must be continually guarded and occasionally revisited for clarification. Regular staff evaluations should include a values-oriented component. This will allow the church to reward and encourage those who are demonstrating the desired values and discipline or to remove those who are failing to do so. Hiring or recruiting should also include prescreening for such values in officer and ministry leadership selection. Maintaining high standards of accountability among current leaders also will contribute to preserving worthy values and reshaping those that require change.

As for changing "what we do" values and "how we do ministry" values, two suggestions come to mind. First, make sure resources are sufficiently aligned with your church's values. Such resources include prime-time activities, leadership, and finances. For instance, a church's leadership may declare outreach to be a "what we do" value but fail to offer outreach training or outreach events during prime time on the church's calendar. This is certain to undermine the stated values. Selecting influential staff or members to lead the ministries that enhance the values and budgeting for their success are ways to turn a value written on paper into a value the church embraces.

All leadership ministry decisions should align with the stated values. Many good ministries have been discontinued or rejected at Perimeter merely because they did not match our "what we do" or "how we do ministry" values. Those decisions were not judgments on the merits of the ministries but expressions of commitment to a clear set of prioritized values. One of the reasons we identify and prioritize values is to aid us in decision making when so many worthwhile opportunities come our way. Without clearly defined priorities to which we maintain faithfulness, our efforts as a church become splintered, chaotic, and ineffective.

In chapter 13 we will address infrastructure. But since we are talking about values in this chapter, let me say now that churches need to design their infrastructure around a multiple-value philosophy. There is always the temptation to allow past ministry successes, a pastor's spiritual gift or talent, or programmatic tradition to elevate a single value to dominate others (especially in the "what we do" values). The American Protestant church has been guilty of this for the last several decades. In my opinion, one "what we do" value has dominated the American Protestant church. That value governs the church's prime time and consumes its best leadership.

In our Inquirer's Class for newcomers, I routinely ask those in attendance to guess which in a list of values they think has been dominant in Protestant churches in recent decades. I take a hand vote before I tell them my choice. Invariably, my first selection is their last. Let's try it with you. Here is a list of "what we do" values:

- Worship and prayer
- Outreach
- Discipleship
- Education
- Fellowship

- Pastoral care
- Service and mercy

Which of these would you say has been the dominant value? If you picked education, you are one of the rare persons who agrees with me. My conviction begs a question, of course: If education has been the dominating value in Protestant churches, then why are so many church members biblically illiterate? The answer to this question has nothing to do with the dominance of education as a value but with the poor quality of education.

My argument for suggesting that education has been the dominant value is simple—look at the church's use of prime-time and primary leadership. In years past, if you were asked to evaluate the worship service, your response was determined primarily by the quality of the sermon (which typically takes one-half of the allotted time). If you attended Sunday school, your evaluation of it was based on the content of the lesson. If you went to Sunday evening church, your impression would be that most of the hour was devoted to teaching by the senior pastor. If you attended Wednesday night prayer meeting, your experience was probably like mine. Almost the entire evening was spent hearing the same senior pastor do the same thing—teach. The meeting then closed with a few people praying for the sick and shut-ins. With all the prime times filled with teaching and the pastor's weekly schedule filled with preparing messages, it is easy to see why education became the dominant value. Little time or leadership was left for service and mercy, prayer, or discipleship.

In the modern lives of our families, prime time is dominated by schedules that are as complex as many small business enterprises. For millions of Americans the pace of life can be exhausting. Busy schedules and fast-paced lives place an enormous challenge on a church that desires a multiple-value philosophy of ministry. Get ready for some extremely hard choices. If one is pitted against the other (and in some respects they often are), which would you choose for your church:

- To be huge or holy?
- To worship or to do outreach?
- To have fellowship or education?
- To offer pastoral care or discipleship?

Certainly, defining the church's values is a challenging yet vital exercise. Later, when we talk about a strategically designed infrastructure, we will walk through this exercise. But for now, know that determining the church's values and listing their priorities is an absolutely indispensable assignment for the church's leadership.

7

Inside the Effective Ministry Plan

5. WELL-DEFINED MISSION

KEY QUESTION

—⁓—

HOW WILL WE
ACHIEVE OUR
VISION?

Imagine you have just accepted a new position that requires you to move your family to a new city. As you walk through the house that has been your home for many years, you're amazed by the amount of stuff that has been collected over the years. You begin to consider your family's future, and soon you recognize a vision for your family: *Relocate and establish firm roots for our family in the new city.*

When you step back and think about it, achieving this vision requires that you break the vision down into distinct, big-picture tasks that need to be completed:

- Identify and hire Realtors.
- Take a family house-hunting trip.
- Hold a garage sale.
- Arrange for movers.
- Finally, identify a church home.

In this example, the five big-picture task statements represent the mission statement and answer the question: "How will we accomplish our vision?" In the context of your church, as you craft your mission statement, it should begin to bring into focus how you will accomplish the vision that God has given you.

That's a major challenge in accepting an "unless God be in it" vision for your church: not being overwhelmed when you begin to think how you will achieve your vision. The first step is to develop the mission statement, which breaks the vision statement into more manageable, big-picture component parts.

THE MISSION STATEMENT: BREAKING THE VISION STATEMENT INTO MANAGEABLE PARTS

The rest of the chapter looks at vision and the resulting mission statement through one church. We believe there are enough applications to other churches as well. At the heart of every intentional church is a specific vision with an accompanying mission statement.

For example, at Perimeter we had to answer the question, "How will we accomplish our vision: 'to bring the people of greater Atlanta and all places we serve into a life-transforming encounter with the kingdom of God'?" We answered this question with the following mission statement:

We will achieve our vision by creating healthy missional communities that accomplish the following:

1. Making mature and equipped followers of Christ
2. Becoming a church of compassion comprised of praying believers willing to give themselves away for the cause of the least and the lost
3. Building strategic bridges between our church and the communities in which we live, work, and play
4. Planting new churches and partnering with existing churches across Atlanta and around the world to strategically do the above

The first statement, "Making mature and equipped followers of Christ," defines the transformation that we are working to bring about in the lives of our people. It is the foundation upon which everything else is built. It is a critical component of the "safe home" role of the church that was discussed in chapter 1. Our success at fulfilling this statement is directly related to our ability to achieve statements 2, 3, and 4. Our success at helping transform an unchurched person into a mature and equipped follower of Christ is directly related to the effectiveness of our outreach, to the effectiveness of shepherding members of our church, to the number of people serving within the church, to the relationships between husbands and wives, and mobilizing people to serve in community and to support and serve in global outreach.

Though the majority of church leaders are likely to agree that the effectiveness of disciple making is foundational to the church, it is my opinion that the present-day church has, for the most part, embraced an ineffective plan for making mature and equipped followers of Christ. This is a discovery that we made about our own ministry. In chapter 8, I will discuss how our church discovered this deficiency and the steps that we have taken to fulfill this critical statement.

The second statement, "Becoming a church of compassion comprised of praying believers willing to give themselves away for the cause of the least and the lost," speaks to our commitment to become a church that has compassion for those in our community that are among the least and the lost. The idea that we are willing to give ourselves away speaks to the fact that we are consciously and intentionally looking for effective ways to give ourselves away.

The third statement, "Building strategic bridges between our church and the communities in which we live, work, and play," is a key component of the second overarching role of the church, "effective mission" (community outreach), which was discussed in chapter 1.

Early in the life of the church, our primary outreach strategy was equipping our people to share their faith with family, friends, and coworkers. Corporately, we supported personal evangelism with a number of outreach events where members could invite their friends. The strategy of personal evangelism supported with churchwide outreach events resulted in many people coming to Christ. Although we were successfully reaching people for Christ, something was missing.

In evaluating our strategies, I looked at the example of Jonathan Edwards and found that the most effective churches emphasize three areas: "the head," which is good theology and a biblical foundation; "the heart," or a passion for worship and for reaching the lost;

and "the hand," meeting needs in our community. What hit me was that we had a good combination of "head and heart," but we were really missing "the hand," meeting needs within the community.

PROVIDING A "HAND" TO THE COMMUNITY

At about the same time that we were evaluating our role to reach out and provide a "hand" to the community, I had an opportunity to read *The Church of Irresistible Influence,* by Robert Lewis. This is a book that I highly recommend. One of its questions had a great impact on me: "If your church was gone tomorrow, would the community notice or care?" What a powerful and challenging statement. Here we are, churches called by God to be transformational agents in our communities, and the reality is that many of our churches, including the church God has called me to lead, are faced with the reality that the majority of people in our communities might not even miss us if we were gone.

I don't want to leave you with the impression that we didn't have any people or ministries reaching out and serving within the community. Like many other churches, we had a number of ministries that were involved in the community. There were also people from our congregation serving with outreach ministries. Our problem was that we were not intentional about praying for and reaching out to meet the needs of people in the community. We didn't have a plan. As a result, we were not only missing opportunities to show our faith through our deeds, we were also missing the opportunity to build relationships that would lead to opportunities to share the good news of Jesus Christ.

Our plan for increasing the impact of our outreach into the community included two key elements. The first was to develop a laity-led ministry supported by staff to equip and mobilize people within the church to use their gifts to serve within the community. The second was that we would connect our people with other ministries, churches, and government agencies within the community that already had an effective track record for meeting needs within the community. One of the most important criteria for selecting our partners was that they would permit our members to be active in both "word and deed" ministry. Our goal in this community outreach ministry is that our members would pray for and be sensitive to the Holy Spirit's leading for opportunities to share the gospel message with the people they are serving.

This approach to ministry has achieved a number of goals:

- Making mature and equipped followers of Christ
- Showing the love of Christ to the individuals whom we have served and the community at large
- Reaching people for Christ

PLANTING AND PARTNERING

The fourth item in our mission statement, "Planting new churches and partnering with existing churches across Atlanta and around the world to strategically do the above," speaks to two distinct strategies for bringing about community transformation in the Atlanta area: (1) planting churches and (2) partnering with other churches.

This statement also speaks to our strategy for global outreach.

To illustrate the development of strategies in support of a vision, I have included summaries for each of the areas noted above and the strategies that we have developed here at Perimeter Church. While they are only summaries, you can get more information on our Web site for each of the areas. The Web site for this information is: www.lifeonlife.org.

Community Transformation Through Church Planting

Church planting has been part of the vision and mission of Perimeter Church since it was first planted approximately thirty years ago. Though our passion for planting has not diminished over the years, our method for planting churches has evolved. Our initial church planting strategy was effectively summarized by the phrase "One church, many congregations."

Following this strategy, we would birth a new congregation from the original church and plant a new church in a rented facility five to ten miles from the original church. I maintained the primary teaching responsibilities at the original church and the new congregation for a period of time. Each Sunday I would preach at the original church and then drive to the new congregation, preach a service, and then return to the original church to preach at the second service.

While the "one church, many congregations" model worked well for planting four congregations, when we began discussing a fifth congregation, we realized that we had reached the limits of this model. After many months of prayer, meetings, and deliberations that included input from a very well-known and highly gifted consultant, we created a new vehicle to advance our vision. We named it Perimeter Ministries International (PMI).

PMI's goal was to accomplish the three tasks the "one church, many congregations" had been doing as a combined ministry:

1. Plant and serve new churches.
2. Direct combined resources from the multiple congregations to enable effective ministry to the underresourced and urban areas of Atlanta.
3. Broker ministries and materials throughout our congregations so as to enhance the effectiveness of each congregation.

Within a year, each of the four congregations of Perimeter Church became organized churches ("particularized"), and the assistant pastor at each congregation became the senior pastor. With the exception of the original church, each church renamed itself to eliminate confusion.

After ten years of being one church, many congregations, we were now four churches. Under this new structure, we immediately began to plant new churches. We quickly found our new arrangement made it much easier to start churches reaching different people groups.

The PMI model served us well for a span of about ten years and we planted more than twenty new churches. PMI was an important component of our mission of bringing transformation to greater Atlanta. However, we found ourselves asking how we could have greater impact in bringing Atlanta and all areas where we serve into a life-transforming encounter with the kingdom of God.

After much prayer, discussion, and evaluation we came to the conclusion to disband PMI. Our commitment to planting churches did not diminish, but we decided that a new model was needed to take us to the next level. We call this new model the Church Planter in Residence.

Church Planter in Residence is a two-year process in which a church planter joins and serves as a full-time, paid member of the

Perimeter staff. One of the key goals of this ministry is to help church planters gain an understanding of Perimeter's vision, mission, strategies, and plans and to see and experience firsthand how these plans are carried out in day-to-day ministry operations.

As I write this, we are at the point of releasing our first Church Planter in Residence "graduates" to plant new churches. We are excited about the impact that these church planters will have on the lives of the people in the local community that God has called them to serve. While we believe that this strategy has the ability to serve us for the next ten years or more, we will evaluate the success and impact of this strategy and modify it or start over if necessary to ensure that we are successfully planting transformational churches.

Reaching Greater Atlanta Through Church Partnering and Unite!

Our church partnering strategy came about as a result of evaluating our church planting strategies in the context of fulfilling our vision: "to bring the people of greater Atlanta and all places we serve into a life-transforming encounter with the kingdom of God." As we evaluated our plans, we came to realize that even if we were blessed to plant another forty churches and reached a total of sixty-four church plants with each serving 1,500 members, we would only be reaching 96,000 people across the greater Atlanta metro area. Even if we were to make a totally unrealistic assumption that the metro area population would stay static at four million people during the next twenty years, that would give us a total reach of less than 3 percent of the metro area. We would be hard-pressed to say that we were achieving our vision for Atlanta.

Convinced that our vision to reach greater Atlanta was God's vision for the church, we realized that church planting alone would not allow us to reach greater Atlanta with the result of transformation.

God is faithful in providing the means when He provides the vision, and we are faithful in pursuing the vision He has provided. We firmly believe that it was God who opened the doors and helped us see the wisdom and strategic importance of partnering with other churches that shared our vision for reaching our city. From this vision a movement called Unite! was born.

Unite! grew out of monthly meetings with Hopewell Baptist

Church, an African-American church located about fifteen minutes from our church. At these meetings, staff from our two churches gathered to pray for our churches and communities and to discuss issues facing our ministries and ideas on how we might address these issues.

The seed of the idea for Unite! came from Lewis's book, *The Church of Irresistible Influence*. In chapter 9, "Joining with Other Churches," Lewis described their inaugural ShareFest in Arkansas, in which one hundred churches across Little Rock joined together in prayer on a Saturday morning, followed with acts of community service that visibly demonstrated the love of God, and then gathered for a time of celebration.

WITH "COMPASSION IN ACTION" . . . WE MOBILIZED CHURCHES FOR MEANINGFUL, HIGHLY VISIBLE WORKS OUTSIDE THE FOUR WALLS OF THE CHURCH.

Our two churches made a commitment to join together to form a core leadership group to develop plans to mobilize churches in northeast Atlanta to pray, serve, and celebrate together. After a short period of time, our group of two churches expanded to a leadership team of seven churches praying and working together. Our first event was a weekend event called "Compassion in Action," in which we mobilized churches for meaningful, highly visible works outside the four walls of the church. Our plan was to hold a celebration event, which we called "Heaven on Earth Celebration," the following weekend.

After months of prayer and hard work, almost 4,500 people from approximately thirty churches came together under the Unite! umbrella to put their love into action by working on a wide range of community projects that had been identified by the participating Unite! churches. These projects included cleaning up and renovating community parks, making improvements to school playgrounds and facilities, blood drives, medical services, block parties at apartment complexes, visiting and providing help at area elder-care centers, home and apartment renovations, home repairs, serving the homeless, working in youth prison, and helping local food pantries.

One of the most important accomplishments of Unite! 2003 is that it laid a foundation for ongoing partnerships in which a growing number of churches across the northeast quadrant of Atlanta could come together to pray, serve, and celebrate.

Currently, seventy churches are a part of Unite! Members of these churches serve with one of the more than thirty-two ministries, non-profit groups, or government agencies that have been identified and screened by Unite!'s participating member churches.

The success of Unite! has helped underscore that even though no one church has the ability to reach a city the size of Atlanta, when seventy-five to one hundred churches partner together across Atlanta, they can begin to have a significant impact on the city. This partnering strategy is compatible with our mission of reaching Atlanta and is an excellent supplement to our church-planting strategy.

GLOBAL OUTREACH

Global outreach through world missions has been a part of the vision and mission of Perimeter from the very beginning of the church's existence. During our early years of ministry, our goal was to reach a point where 50 percent of our budget would support work outside of Perimeter and fulfill the Acts 1:8 command to be Christ's "witnesses in Jerusalem, and in all Judea and Samaria, and to the ends of the earth." Our goal was to use the majority of these resources to support world missions.

During the mid-1990s we made a significant shift in our global outreach strategy. As we reviewed the missions movement on a global level, a new understanding of how Perimeter could best serve the needs of our targeted areas began to emerge. We shifted our emphasis to supporting and serving indigenous ministries.

The initial reaction of most people is to look at our mission statement (how we plan to accomplish our vision) and draw the conclusion that our global outreach ministry fulfills the fourth point of our mission. However, our global outreach ministry is a critical component for fulfilling the first three points as well: (1) making mature and equipped followers of Christ; (2) becoming a church of compassion comprised of praying believers willing to give themselves away for the cause; and (3) building strategic bridges between our church and the communities in which we live.

We believe that a person maturing as a follower of Christ will have a heart for global outreach and fulfilling the Great Commission and the Acts 1:8 command to take the gospel to all the world. To that end we have made it possible for our members to be involved through prayer, personally participating in journeys, working with our international partners and seeing firsthand the measurable transformation that is taking place in targeted villages, cities, or countries.

Just as in our ministry efforts here in Atlanta, in our global outreach we are focused on the concept of "measurable transformation." Our first expectation is that our partners will see transformation in the lives of people within the church through effective disciple making. As they successfully mobilize disciples for ministry outside the church, they will see measurable community transformation. As the gospel goes forth and men and women are becoming mature and equipped followers of Christ, we anticipate seeing overall improvements in the quality of life spiritually, economically, socially, and medically.

I am convinced that our global outreach strategy is one of our best kept secrets here at Perimeter Church. The work that God has done in those areas where we are partnering is incredible. The work that God has done in the lives of our members is as equally amazing. Churches are being planted, pastors are being trained, laypeople are being reached with the Good News and discipled, and the hope that comes with the Good News is filling hearts around the world.

DEVELOPING *YOUR* MISSION STATEMENT

Thank you for indulging me as I have spotlighted some of the ministry activities at Perimeter Church. I know that ministry in your context will look very different. My desire is to show you that a compelling God-given vision must work itself into mission statements that will allow each church to accomplish its unique vision. While we believe that God has called Perimeter to have an impact on the greater Atlanta area and all areas where we serve, His vision for your church may be very different.

The important thing to keep in mind in developing your mission statement is that you identify and define the three to five statements that effectively describe the big-picture strategies that, when taken together, will help move you toward fulfilling the vision that God has given to your church.

I personally believe one of the ways you will know that you are on track in the development of your vision and mission is that your church's mission will include statements that define the *transformations* you are seeking to bring about *in* the lives of your people as well as *through* the lives of your people.

8

Inside the Mission

ACCOMPLISHING VISION BY MAKING MATURE, EQUIPPED FOLLOWERS OF CHRIST

As I stated in the previous chapter, it is my opinion that the present-day church has, for the most part, embraced an ineffective plan for making mature and equipped followers of Christ. As we evaluated our own ministry at Perimeter Church, we discovered two things. First, while we were throwing around terms such as *trained disciples, mature believers, and equipped Christians,* we did not have an agreed-upon definition for such people. Second, after arriving at a definition for making a mature and equipped disciple, we discovered that our program-based approach was limited in its ability to make mature disciples.

DEFINITION OF A DISCIPLE

As mentioned in chapter 1, early in our ministry our elders agreed that we would consider our church a safe home when our people were routinely provided with the following:

- Vital worship that demonstrates the presence and power of God
- True fellowship founded in significant and meaningful relationships
- Biblical instruction and discipleship training grounded in biblical theology
- Pastoral care and shepherding directed toward the needs of the whole person
- Equipping and empowering to do the work of ministry

These criteria served us for many years. They provided helpful guidelines as we evaluated the effectiveness of our work at equipping the people of our church. All well and good—but eventually someone raised the question, "What kind of 'residents' do you expect to produce as a result of these guidelines?" The variety of answers that we gave only proved one thing: We had a lot of ideas but no clear ideal. We had never clearly identified what the "residents" of our church should, in time, look like.

What Are "Mature and Equipped Followers of Christ"?

I can think of few healthier exercises in our church's life than when we wrestled with this issue and developed a working description. Until this time, it had been easy to hit our vision's bull's-eye—simply shoot the arrow and draw a circle around wherever it hit! We had been focused almost entirely on the process without having a clear target. It was at this time we agreed the residents we would seek to develop would be called "mature and equipped followers of Christ."

Using that phrase, we have developed a clear outline of measurable expectations regarding the kind of believers we desire to produce. A mature and equipped follower of Christ is one who:

- lives consistently under the control of the Holy Spirit, the direction of the Word of God, and the compelling love of Christ;
- has discovered, developed, and is using his or her spiritual gifts;
- has learned to effectively share his or her faith while demonstrating radical love that amazes the world it touches; and
- gives strong evidence of being:
  - a faithful member of God's church,
  - an effective manager of life, relationships, and resources,

- a willing minister to God's people, and
- an available messenger to nonkingdom people.

In addition, the mature, equipped follower of Christ demonstrates a life characterized as

- gospel driven
- morally pure
- discipleship grounded
- socially responsible
- worship focused
- evangelistically bold
- family faithful

Though your wording will differ, I believe that the definition of a disciple is one of the most critical elements of the development of your plan. It defines the life change that your church is working to bring about in the lives of your people. It is through these changed lives that you will achieve your God-given vision for your church.

A Perspective on Maturity

Over the years, I have observed a faulty assumption in the church at large regarding maturity. The majority report among Christians seems to be that Christian maturity is measured by the biblical and theological knowledge a person has assembled coupled with his spiritual commitment. Yet I am amazed how little emphasis is given to the observable life change that is brought about by the application of Scripture to their lives. Now I know that behavior alone does not declare someone to be mature. Only God knows the motives of a person's heart. But our own Master told us we would determine if a person is one of His followers simply by observing his fruit. Certainly our judgment of such fruit can be faulty and even differ from one observer to the next. Yet fruit is nevertheless an indication of genuine maturity.

I am also amazed at how many people consider themselves mature in Christ but cannot identify anyone who has entered the kingdom because of their life and witness. This is not to suggest that the number of people who come to Christ through an individual's personal witness is a measure of the person's spiritual maturity. It is the Holy Spirit working in the life of the person who hears the message that results in a person coming to faith in Christ. We are called to be faithful in sharing the gospel while depending on the Holy Spirit to produce the fruit.

The guidelines above are primarily designed to help the believer evaluate his own maturity and give the church a reasonable measuring rod to evaluate its work in presenting people "complete [mature] in Christ" (Colossians 1:28).

AN INEFFECTIVE PLAN

Many churches embrace the goal of making mature and equipped followers of Christ. Most would summarize their plan for doing so in this way: "by providing sound biblical teaching and beneficial, need-oriented programs." In fact, this was Perimeter Church's practice for years. Like many of these churches, we also used two seldom-examined questions to measure our success at being an effective "home":

- How many people came to hear the truth?
- How well was the truth presented?

Such self-examination questions need some attention here. Do these two questions really tell us what we need to know? The first of these questions does provide a measurable result. If "exposure to good teaching and a variety of learning opportunities" summarizes an effective method, then attendance figures indicate success or failure. This standard presupposes that exposure measures effectiveness. But does it actually do so?

One way to test the usefulness of such a question is to apply it to the ministry of Jesus. Was Jesus' effectiveness really determined by the multitudes that showed up for His teaching? Or did He use a different standard (see Matthew 7:24–27)? The crowds who merely heard His words didn't impress Him; He was looking for those who would hear and put His teaching into practice.

The second question, "How well was the truth presented?" invites a subjective evaluation. "How well" seldom means "how faithful to the truth" or "how effective was the presentation in terms of motivating application and life change." It usually means "how interesting, how contemporary, and how varied." The term I now use to describe a church with this approach is *program-based*. A church is program-based when its primary method of making mature and equipped followers of Christ centers on the delivery of truth through the vehicles of church programs (for example, seminars, preaching, and classes).

I have already admitted my growing skepticism about the ability of the traditional or contemporary church of today to accomplish the goal of making mature and equipped followers of Christ. For many years my hope lay in the new emphasis on small-group ministry. Our church was one of the pioneers in this movement, only to realize that most small groups eventually become primarily "care and share" fellowship groups and Bible studies. Though much good came from this emphasis, it still seemed to me to ultimately miss the goal of the church. This is not to say that small groups cannot produce mature and equipped followers of Christ. Rather, it is to admit that most churches, ours included, did not structure our small groups with this end specifically in mind. The means got confused with the ends. We assumed that small groups *somehow* automatically led to maturity.

We eventually had to admit that small groups simply represented another program in a program-based approach to church. We came to the painful realization that small groups and other merely program-based approaches would not in themselves accomplish either our vision or our mission—not because we didn't have enthusiastic and growing small groups but because our small groups failed to produce mature and equipped followers of Christ.

I came to this conclusion on a summer study leave and discussed my concerns with our elder board. They could have chosen rapid growth over faithfulness. After all, judged by program-based questions, we were doing very well. Instead, the elders urged me to take whatever time necessary to develop a plan that would make our church's lifestyle and structure compatible with the desired product (mature and equipped followers of Christ). Allow me to tell the story of that pilgrimage.

BEYOND PROGRAMS TO WHAT?

I began my quest with our church staff. I trust this special group of men and women. They are deeply committed to our vision and our values. Early in our discussion one of our staff raised an intriguing question: "Well, who are the mature and equipped believers in our church?" As we began creating a list, we saw an interesting pattern developing. We realized that some of the most mature followers of Christ in our body were men I had personally discipled. I had the privilege of leading many of them to Christ. Most had, at some point, been part of the small group I was leading. That first discovery led to the next logical question: "What do you do with these guys when you disciple them?" It was the answer to this question that ultimately set our ministry in a new direction.

Until this time, I didn't realize I had been doing anything all that unusual. My approach to discipleship was a combination of ideas and methods that had impacted my own life as a believer:

- I made sure the men I worked with were learning *the truth*. In addition to personal teaching sessions, I assigned them tapes to listen to and books and Bible texts to read.
- I spent time *equipping* them—showing them how to use the truths they had learned. I describe this process as "massaging the truth until it becomes understandable and usable." For instance, I learned I couldn't stop once I "taught" them how to personally worship. I had to actually "walk with them" through worship. I needed to show them how to worship and then lead them in worship.
- I insisted that our relationship in discipleship include a significant ingredient of *accountability*—asking hard questions and challenging bad behavior.
- I emphasized and personalized *mission*—targeting a people group or list of individuals we were in the process of trying to reach with the gospel.
- I prayed (*supplication*) regularly for each man in my group and they prayed for each other. We also spent time each week praying together as a group.

As we looked at these components, we saw an acrostic emerge that became a descriptive title for a new approach to ministry that was embraced churchwide at Perimeter. Taking the first letter of each of the five key words—*truth, equipping, accountability, mission,* and *supplication*—we spelled the word TEAMS. We began calling our new paradigm of ministry TEAMS-based ministry. With every passing year of ministry I have become more deeply convinced that these five ingredients are indispensable in making mature and equipped followers of Christ.

THE VALUE OF "SITUATIONAL LEADERSHIP"

Not long after this exercise with our staff, I attended a pastors' forum where business consultant and author Ken Blanchard was speaking. Ken described the adjustment phases that a person experiences in progressing from a new employee to a veteran and dependable partner. As he introduced his situational leadership concept, I discovered unexpected outside confirmation that we were headed in the right direction. Ken has written about this leadership structure in *Leadership and the One Minute Manager: Increasing Effectiveness Through Situational Leadership* (coauthored by Patricia Zigarmi and Drea Zigarmi).[1] Since you may not be familiar with this concept, let me briefly describe it.

Blanchard begins with the first need of a new learner (whether a new employee or a church member). He or she must be given clear instructions and directives. But if this learner is typical, he then needs hands-on coaching to show him how to use his newly acquired directives. Next, his need progresses to simply requiring support. He no longer needs the direct coaching but feels much more secure knowing that a coach is nearby, if necessary. In time, this learner becomes so confident and competent that he can be delegated any duty in his area of expertise. In fact, once he is ready for delegation, he is likely to view any attempt to direct, coach, or support him as undesirable and unnecessary.

"A MODEL OF SITUATIONAL LEADERSHIP"

2 Coaching	3 Supporting
Directing 1	Delegating 4

Source: Adapted from Kenneth H. Blanchard, Patricia Zigarmi, and Drea Zigarmi, *Leadership and the One Minute Manager: Increasing Effectiveness Through Situational Leadership* (New York: William Morrow, 1984), 47.

On the other hand, taking a learner straight from accepting basic direction to handling delegation is likely to produce, at best, a disillusioned learner. As I listened to Ken's description of these developmental steps, I couldn't help but realize their application in the church.

In fact, if any institution is guilty of violating situational leadership, it has to be the church. For example, we preach to new Christians about the importance and how-tos of evangelism and then close the message by delegating the task to them. We describe evangelism and then say, "Do it!" Young Christians frequently charge into the world with the best intentions of sharing their faith only to fail miserably. Witnessing seldom turns out the way it was described in the motivating message. These new believers become disillusioned learners, believing that something is uniquely wrong with them. They then vow never to go through that experience again. The next sermon on evangelism becomes little more than a whipping rod, producing guilt.

As I reflected further on Blanchard's comments, the genius behind TEAMS-based ministry became apparent to me. The truth we teach new believers fit Blanchard's definition of directives. Effective equipping is the same as coaching. Accountability falls into the category of support, and mission is the essence of delegation. New believers need to be taught the truth and they eventually need to "do it" themselves, but there are significant steps between their starting point and their development into mature and equipped believers.

DIVING IN

Several years ago I decided to surprise my oldest son, Matt, with a high school graduation present he would never expect. I gave him scuba diving lessons and told him we would get certified together. Because of my erratic schedule, I arranged for us to take private lessons to allow more flexibility. After selecting the instructor, I learned that the standard procedure was to spend half of each weekly training session in the classroom and half in an indoor diving pool. Realizing I had an upcoming, lengthy trip to Asia, I asked permission to front-load our classroom time and, in fact, to allow us to do that portion in a self-directed study format. In other words, we would take the materials, study them without lectures, and be tested on our knowledge of diving. The instructor reluctantly agreed but assured us that our test results would have to be exceptional.

For several weeks during my Asia trip I studied diligently. I quickly discovered I knew nothing of scuba diving. I had assumed this sport was simple. You jumped into the water with a hose in your mouth and sucked real hard. Little did I comprehend the risks in this activity. As I began reading my manual, I repeatedly came across such words as *danger, life threatening,* and *serious injury.* For instance, I learned that due to changing pressures at different depths, the diver must ascend slowly and that at approximately thirty feet of depth must "hold" for three to five minutes to reestablish appropriate nitrogen levels in the body. To rush immediately to the surface could be deadly. This warning, however, only gave me slight worry. I still thought the directions were clear, obvious, and simple. Having completed our self-directed study, Matt and I took our exams and passed easily. Now it was time to get wet!

The first week of pool instruction was spent getting acquainted with the diving equipment and practicing distress maneuvers. After learning to clear our masks and use a snorkel and regulator, we were ready to role-play.

Our instructor explained that we would go to the bottom of the twelve-foot pool and operate as "diving buddies"—committed to helping one another in time of difficulty. He described our first test. After we were resting on the pool floor he would randomly point at one of us, indicating the partner in distress. At that time the victim diver was to immediately remove his regulator from his mouth, give the distress signal (arms crossing above the head), and indicate "out of air" (hand motion across the neck). The instructor also spelled out several conditions: (1) We could not abandon the mission. (2) The one in distress could not grab the partner's second stage (the backup regulator). (3) Instead, he was to wait for his partner to place it appropriately in his mouth, allow time to get stabilized, and then slowly proceed to the top. Everything seemed so simple!

Moments later, as Matt and I rested at the bottom of the pool, the instructor pointed to me. In a second, the atmosphere of absolute calm was exchanged for a rush of nervous excitement. Unfortunately, the signal came just as I had ended a long, slow exhale in my regulator. Without thinking, I spit out the regulator while my lungs were completely empty. Realizing my urgent need for air, I gave a very quick distress signal and an out-of-air signal in order to communicate to my son that we needed to speed up the process.

Well, if you knew my son, you would know that he's never been in a hurry in his life—and this time was no exception! He seemed to look casually at me, glance at his backup regulator, and think, *I guess you need some air.* From my breathless perspective, too much time had already elapsed, so I did the unpardonable—I reached out to grab Matt's backup regulator. The instructor immediately and rudely slapped my hand away from Matt's vest. At this point, I decided enough was enough. I pushed up from the pool floor so as to surface and get some much-needed air.

MY SON AND I GRADUALLY MOVED FROM THE STAGE OF DIRECTIVES . . . TO COACHING . . . TO SUPPORT . . . TO DELEGATION.

Just as my head was about to break the water surface, the instructor grabbed my legs and pulled me back to the bottom. The role-play had become painful reality! My lungs were now about to explode. Finally, Matt was kind enough to give me his second regulator, and we returned to the surface. After graciously chewing me out, my instructor explained how serious such a move would have been had we been one hundred feet below the surface. I shamefacedly nodded in agreement. But the lecture failed to penetrate my inexperienced confidence. I was still sure that I could quickly master this simple sport.

After several weeks of instruction, the time finally came for our deepwater dives and certification evaluation. Our dive site was several miles off the Florida coast. The first dive took us briefly down to thirty feet. Next we descended to sixty feet. The third of seven dives found us at the maximum depth for amateur diving, one hundred feet. We rehearsed our plan to stay down for the allotted time and then at the instructor's signal to slowly ascend, holding for five minutes at thirty feet before surfacing.

At the end of our "bottom time" on this third dive, our instructor signaled us to begin our ascent. At approximately thirty feet he gave us notice to "hold." Though I fully intended to stop at thirty feet, I suddenly realized I couldn't control my ascent. In my inexperience, I didn't realize I had a pocket of air trapped in my vest. It was rocketing to the surface and taking me with it. Once again, my instructor found himself in that all too familiar position of hanging on to my legs. This time, however, he was unable to pull me down. We were both unwillingly carried upward. As we broke the surface, we both grabbed our heads, suffering an unhealthy lightheadedness.

I had done exactly what my instruction manual warned could be life threatening.

Once we were back on the boat we evaluated what had happened. We rehearsed how to avoid the same problem the next time. Then we waited on the ship's deck while we accrued our "surface time," the required period between dives. Meanwhile, I was anxious about the upcoming fourth dive. My self-confidence had been humbled.

As we entered the water the fourth time, I was amazingly conscious of the whereabouts of the instructor. I wanted him right next to me at all times. Dives four and five proceeded without trouble. By our last two dives, we had spearguns in hand, chasing fish, mindless of any fears or concerns. In fact, the dive instructor's proximity gradually became a nuisance to me. It would not have bothered me if he had left us at one hundred feet and gone back to the boat. I was now sufficiently equipped.

This story illustrates well the TEAMS process. My son and I gradually moved from the stage of directives (learning the "truth" about diving), to coaching (offering "equipping" beneath the water), to support (having my instructor by my side offering the "accountability" I needed to provide me security), to delegation (sending me into the deep on a diving "mission" accompanied by confidence based on experience). After this, the instructor was "prayerfully" available from a distance for further training, counsel, and delegation.

Can you imagine after dive number three being told to go down to one hundred feet without the instructor? The problems on that dive had finally gotten my undivided attention. I realized that testing well on the content of the training hadn't been enough. My accumulation of knowledge, though it was the truth, did not negate my desperate need for coaching and accountability from my instructor. Yet this truth is exactly what the church is notorious for ignoring. We give our people directives (truth) and then delegate the task (mission) of living for Christ and serving Him without the necessary equipping and accountability.

What does it take to go from a definition of making disciples to building followers of Christ who are mature in Him and equipped for His business? I like the phrase *life-on-life investment*, which we will discuss in more detail in chapter 20. We can have state-of-the-art educational wings; we can have DVD players and PowerPoint presentations and a parade of guest speakers dispensing truth. Such environments do much for making knowledgeable Christians but do little in the effort to create mature and equipped followers of Christ. We gravitate to these environments and methods because they deal with groups, but let me repeat: effective discipleship requires a patient, time-consuming life-on-life personal commitment.

Note

1. Kenneth H. Blanchard, Patricia Zigarmi, and Drea Zigarmi, *Leadership and the One Minute Manager: Increasing Effectiveness Through Situational Leadership* (New York: William Morrow, 1984).

9

Inside the Mission

MAKING MATURE AND EQUIPPED FOLLOWERS: THE T E A M S-BASED CHURCH

With the help of many people, I presented a biblical approach through which I believe the church could accomplish its primary purpose, producing mature and equipped followers of Christ. We introduced the descriptive term TEAMS-based church (as opposed to program-based church). This allowed us to communicate to our church leaders the difference between where we had been as a church and the direction in which we needed to move.

They agreed that our church would be considered TEAMS-based when:

- its primary method of making mature and equipped followers of Christ centers on the use of *Truth, Equipping, Accountability, Mission,* and *Supplication;* and
- its primary outreach, nurture, education, care, discipline, and equipping take place in small groups where the leader is

considered the pastor and the community out of which the participants come (residential, relational, professional, or social) is considered the mission field.

The contrasts between the program-based church and the TEAMS-based church are considerable. The differences summarized below are only a few.

Program-Based Church	TEAMS-Based Church
1. Its ministries are mostly *centralized*.	1. Its ministries are mostly *decentralized*.
2. Its effectiveness is evaluated by the quantity and quality of its *ministries*.	2. Its effectiveness is evaluated by the quantity and quality of its *disciples*.
3. Its people ask the question: "What is the *church* doing?"	3. Its people ask the question: "What are *we as believers* doing?"
4. It views the *professional staff* as the pastors.	4. It views the *small-group leaders* as the pastors.
5. Its members are expected to be *consumers*.	5. Its members are expected to be *ministers*.
6. Its small groups function as "homes" that meet the needs of God's people.	6. Its small groups function both as "homes" that meet the needs of God's people, and as "missions" that reach the unchurched communities.
7. Its strategy for making mature believers is *singularly focused* on the delivery of truth.	7. Its strategy for making mature believers is *multifocused* on the requirements of truth, equipping, accountability, mission, and supplication.
8. It places *undue emphasis* on the importance of *teachers*.	8. It places *equal emphasis* on the importance of teachers, pastors, and disciplers.
9. Its *classroom ministry* is more important than its small-group ministry.	9. Its *small-group ministry* is more important than its classroom ministry.
10. Its staff and elders focus primarily on *deciding* and *directing*.	10. Its staff and elders focus primarily on *discipling*, *pastoring*, and *teaching*.

PERSONAL OUTREACH

Who is the church for? This is a tension church leaders continually wrestle with: Do we primarily exist to nurture the sheep within our fold, or do we exist to reach the lost and hurting outside our walls? Many start with the question: Can we do both with equal effectiveness and still be faithful to what Christ has called us to? From our early beginnings, we have believed that the more appropriate question is: How can we do both with equal effectiveness?

The importance of this question was driven home during the time of searching for the answers to how to make mature and equipped followers of Christ. During this process an important insight became extremely clear:

> Unless the church goes beyond being a safe home for God's people and becomes an effective mission to a lost world, there will not be an environment conducive to making mature and equipped followers of Christ.

I define discipleship as "having a life product, being intentional about imparting that product, and spending enough time doing the right things to impart that product." Discipleship must take place on the front lines of mission. People often say they meet weekly to be discipled by someone at a restaurant. I immediately respond by asking if this is where they think discipleship begins and ends.

Discipleship may include a discussion across a restaurant table, but it certainly doesn't end there. Jesus said to those He discipled, "Follow Me." Then He led them into the intensity of battle for God's kingdom, right to the front lines. He watched them fail and coached their efforts. It was there that the disciples began asking the right questions. It was there that the disciples gained perspective in applying the truth that they had been learning on an ongoing basis. Yes, Jesus and His disciples broke bread together at the table, but their shared meals were only a small part of His effort to grow them into mature and equipped followers.

> TO EFFECTIVELY MAKE MATURE FOLLOWERS OF CHRIST, THE CHURCH MUST BE INTENTIONALLY "SCATTERED" THROUGHOUT ITS COMMUNITY.

SCATTERED

Another insight that emerged during the development of the TEAMS process had to do with the means of taking discipling to the front lines of battle. We learned that to effectively make mature and equipped followers of Christ, the church must be intentionally "scattered" throughout its community. We easily think of the church as "gathered" corporately for weekly worship, but we don't have a clear picture of what it means to be a church "scattered." That lack is a clue to the absence of a "mission" (outreach) commitment to complement the "safe home" commitment of the church. If we can't see the church scattered, effective scattering is probably not occurring.

Believers who clearly understand and accept their mission when they walk out of church are the same believers who find their greatest joy and anticipation in gathering for worship again. That's because their mission mind-set gives them many opportunities to see God work, and they are eager to meet again with others who share their commitment. Scattering and gathering complement each other in the life of the church. Without intentional and mission-oriented scattering, the gathering simply becomes a weekly worship and teaching session.

LEARNING FROM OTHER CULTURES

The "world's largest church," Yoido Full Gospel Church in Seoul, South Korea, has been a source of curiosity and amazement because of its size. Its growth has been exponential for years. Why? Because they have taken seriously the task of "scattering" as well as "gathering." But more important, they have kept the task of mission as important as the task of home (even in the church scattered). We see this approach mirrored time and time again, particularly in Asian, Latin American, and South American cultures.

Many American pastors have observed what happens in these other countries and have tried to import the same approach to the United States. They have experienced a high rate of failure. As our staff studied these effective Third World churches, we wondered why such an approach appears to be nontransferable into our culture.

The answer, we believe, lies in the substantial differences between our cultures. Here are a few of those many differences.

1. The High Expectations of American Churchgoers

Americans have been spoiled by high standards of excellence. The people of our churches can turn on their radios and TVs at any time and find brilliant teachers and teaching. Meeting in a home to be taught by a moderately gifted layman pales in comparison. The same is true of music. Yet in many of these foreign cultures any teaching and any music is highly appreciated and embraced.

2. The Simpler, Slower Lifestyles of Other Cultures

The simpler and slower lifestyles of these cultures compared to the prosperity and mobility of America allow for little travel away from home. Leaders and attendees alike have few conflicts with active participation in their home groups. We, in America, might miss two out of four weeks due to various commitments. We live with overbooked calendars.

3. Fewer Alternative Activities and Distractions

These cultures typically provide very few competitive, alternative activities and distractions. In America a house church is just one more choice among many possibilities. Our relational cups can be filled in many different venues. In many foreign cultures, the only social activity of life is found through the church—more like the first half of the twentieth century in America.

4. Submission to God-Given Authorities

People in these cultures more readily submit to God-given authorities. This includes ecclesiastical authority. In talking to a lay pastor of this type of scattered church in Guatemala, I discovered that their house church pastors would not go out of town for their first year of service—not even for vacation. After a year, if an apprentice had been raised up to assist, the lay pastor could ask permission to be absent. Only if allowed would he miss his home church responsibilities.

When I challenged this idea as perhaps a little too heavy-handed, my Guatemalan friend looked at me with a puzzled look. He said, "You are shocked at the respect and obedience demonstrated to our

God-given church leaders who keep watch over our souls; we are shocked at the indiscriminate submission you show to your marketplace bosses. They tell you Monday morning to be in Chicago on Tuesday and you immediately comply, even if you have to miss your kid's championship soccer game on Tuesday afternoon." His point was well made.

A Lesson from South Korea

Church consultant Carl George tells the story of talking to the pastor of Yoido Full Gospel Church, Paul (David) Yonggi Cho. He asked Pastor Cho what the secret was to his church growing by 20 percent each year even after reaching several hundred thousand in size. His answer was quick: "That's simple. You divide your church into groups of ten and require each group to win at least two people to Christ each year."

Carl responded by saying, "Yes, I understand, but what happens when those groups don't win two people a year?" Cho answered, "But they do!"

In dismay Carl said, "But what if a group doesn't win two?"

Pastor Cho immediately responded, "We would discipline them. Jesus said, 'Follow Me and I will make you fishers of men.' If ten people do not win two people over the course of a year, it means they are not following Christ and need to be disciplined."

Pastor Cho's words show the chasm between cultures outside of the American culture. We struggle in America to discipline for sins such as adultery. We are certainly far from disciplining believers for their failure to faithfully evangelize!

The point of these illustrations is not to say we should discipline Christians who fail to share their faith or require our small-group pastors to forfeit vacations or require pastors to get permission from their supervisors when they need to travel. Rather, it is to say that we must recognize the differences in our cultures and humbly seek to identify principles that are transferable. Ministry approaches used in other cultures must be translated before we can expect them to work in ours. Having said that, let me add that we can learn much from our brothers and sisters overseas.

MAKING THE "SCATTERED" CHURCH WORK

In my personal research, six principles have emerged that stand out regarding the success of the church functioning well when scattered. They are:

- Leaders must have no other major responsibilities in the church. To be a pastor or a discipler is a time-consuming ministry for a lay leader.
- The groups must meet at different times for the different functions of "home" and "mission" (as we have seen) in order to keep both clear.
- Prayer and fasting must undergird the decentralized ministry.
- *Good* ministries (often conflicting with the *best* ministries) have to be scaled back.
- Leaders must be equipped weekly and over long periods of time.
- There must be an extensive apprentice-training program.

Our efforts at Perimeter to translate these principles into our own culture, schedules, and appetite turned out to be a challenging process. But we were committed to living out a well-defined mission. More will be discussed later, but let me say that when we began we knew several changes had to take place. Prayer and fasting had to receive greater emphasis in our ministry. Leadership roles had to change. Elders had to move from functioning primarily as directors and decision makers to focusing on pastoring and discipling. We had to redesign the roles of our staff, moving many of them from program oversight to people oversight. This meant describing and hiring new staff positions. We had to call a moratorium on starting new ministries that were competing for resources with such a decentralized ministry. And very important, we had to significantly enhance our leadership training. (More about this when we discuss strategy.)

FIVE PARADIGMS

We can identify five paradigms that the church has embraced over her history. The "gathering-and-scattering" concept (G and S) has to do with *location:* where ministry happens. The "home-and-mission" (H and M) idea has to do with *purpose:* what the ministry is

for. Five boxes illustrate these paradigms, beginning with what I call
the "New Testament Church":

Gathered		Scattered	
H	M	H	M

The New Testament church functioned as both gathered (as a
large community fellowship) and scattered (from house to house).
Throughout the New Testament the church functioned both as a
home (meeting the needs of its people) and as a mission (reaching out
to win the lost). The dynamic of the early church as recorded by Luke
in the Acts of the Apostles is unquestionable. Though maturity might
have been suspect in much of the early church, its zeal and effectiveness was considerable.

Next we move to the "Dark Ages Church."

Gathered			

Notice that the boxes are now empty. Much has changed since
the New Testament Church. Though the church was still gathered,
it was no longer functioning in a scattered capacity. Because the
church had abandoned the truth (for the most part) we have erased
the H. Thus, God's people were not cared for or nurtured. Certainly
the church had no evangelistic zeal; thus, the removal of the M.

Next we come to the "Reformation Church." Great advances
occurred during the Reformation. The most important was that the
Word of God was brought back to the people of God. The church,
though still meeting only as gathered, now brought the function of
home back to the church. God's people could now be taught and fed
the truth. However, the Reformation movement was not known for
its mission to a lost world as much as a ministry to the existing church
(I realize some will disagree with me on this, but allow me to make
the greater point). Thus, our descriptive box looks as follows:

Gathered			
H			

Note how many churches, even today, that embrace the Reformed faith are modeled in this manner. They are most often traditionally gathered only and are satisfied with the task of proclaiming the truth even if there is no evangelistic fruit (even when amidst a productive harvest). Although I fully and proudly embrace the Reformed faith, I am also grieved at the failure in mission so many of our churches experience.

We now move several centuries through time to come to the modern-day church. In the 1970s, a new paradigm in the church began to emerge that would redefine the way church is done. It began with Willow Creek Community Church in a suburb of Chicago and is typically described as the seeker-sensitive church. This church is illustrated as follows:

Gathered			
H	M		

At last, mission was brought back to the church. Willow Creek proved that mission is not the task of only parachurch organizations. It can be done well by the bride of Christ herself. Seekers could be invited into the gathered church and hear the gospel effectively presented there.

Though Willow Creek has in recent years pioneered small-group (scattered) ministry, it has been known more as a church that gathers to do its mission. We call it a "front door church." Even at Willow Creek, I think it is fair to say that most small groups do not scatter for the sake of mission but primarily for the function of home, though this has been changing more in recent years.

Then along came a new model championed by church growth consultant Carl George. It is typically referred to as the Meta-Church—the changing church model. This was Carl's attempt to see the church scattered—his application of lessons in exponential growth learned from the overseas church. This church is depicted as follows:

Gathered		Scattered	
H	M	H	

I know it was Carl's greatest intention to see the church's "scattered" function as both a home and as a mission. I have discussed this at length with him. I know he would disagree with me, but my investigation of the churches used as models of the church as a mission in its decentralization do not prove to be so (from my vantage point). Even as God has used Bill Hybels through Willow Creek, He has also mightily used Carl George to shape the church more into the likeness of God's intentions.

From my perspective, there is one more shift that needs to be made. Adding the "M" of mission to the church scattered is one of the greatest challenges the church faces today. Whether or not this is called a TEAMS-based church is irrelevant; the important thing is that this change gets implemented. When this happens we will actually be functioning in much the same paradigm as the New Testament Church.

Gathered		Scattered	
H	M	H	M

Little did we realize, when we began the journey of trying to answer the question of how to make mature followers of Christ, that we were, in essence, suggesting a radical change in the way church is done. We appreciate the valuable lessons learned from others and are eager to stay faithful to the vision God has given us. The best way we can do that is to make sure that our mission statement clearly outlines a means to achieve our vision.

AN AFTERTHOUGHT

As I noted early in this chapter, I admit to a narrow focus in the historical overview I presented. I wanted to illustrate the general course the church has followed from age to age. God has certainly preserved and extended His church throughout history. Ultimately, the very existence of the church today is first and foremost a tribute to the One who said, "On this rock I will build my church, and the gates of Hades will not overcome it" (Matthew 16:18 NIV).

I am also convinced that in every era, there has been a core within the church that has, in one way or another, preserved the New Testament model of the church. For example, I might mention the Methodist awakening of the eighteenth century, when Anglican clergy such as Whitefield and the Wesleys brought mission, discipleship, and the scattering aspects back to the church. John Wesley, in particular, was painstakingly methodical in his pursuit of discipleship. The principles that we call TEAMS can be clearly seen in what Wesley called his "class meetings." In these highly structured small groups, biblical truth, equipping for ministry, accountability, mission, and supplication were the order of the day.

The urgent question for us is this: What must the church today do in order to live as a New Testament church in our time and place? That challenge must guide us every step of the way.

10

Inside the Effective Ministry Plan

6. BIBLICALLY BASED JOB DESCRIPTIONS— THE ROLES OF DEACONS AND ELDERS

KEY QUESTION

—ɯ—

WHO DOES WHAT?

The leader of one of America's first megachurches correctly defined leadership and its importance when he said: "Leadership is the key to church growth. If the church is really to succeed in its mission of witnessing to the nonchurched world in the twenty-first century, it must develop aggressive, dynamic and inspiring leaders." He then added:

> Leadership is thinking ahead, planning for the future, exhausting all possibilities, envisioning problems and dreaming up solutions to them, and then communicating the possibilities and the problem-solving ideas to the decision makers. This is leadership.
>
> In any institution, the leader is the [person] who is thinking ahead of everyone else. He is not living in the past but in the future, for leadership draws its inspiration from future projections and not from past accomplishments. The leader is alert to movements,

trends and evolving developments. He is literally thinking longer thoughts than anyone else is—and expressing them effectively![1]

At this stage in the development of the strategic plan for your church, you have developed purpose and vision statements. You have developed a mission statement that defines the big picture on how you will achieve your vision. You've also discussed the values of the church and developed a definition of disciples. One of the next steps in the process is to address a crucial piece of the puzzle: Who leads all this?

Question several employees of any successful company regarding who their customer is or who their employer is, and you will get both consistent and accurate answers. Ask a group of faithful members of most churches who the "customer" of their church is, or who serves the roles of employee and employer in the church, and you may well get a different response from every person. Can you imagine a company operating smoothly with this kind of confusion? No wonder so many churches today are ineffective! Clear and well-communicated job descriptions are as important for a church as for a business.

Perhaps the first and most critical issue for a church to settle is to clearly identify the church's leadership and determine how that leadership will function. Though this may sound elementary, it remains an unsettled and disputed issue in many churches.

WHO'S IN CHARGE?

Who should carry out the leadership functions in a church? Is it the pastor, a team of staff leaders, an elder board, or a board of directors? Several other key questions cannot be avoided:

- Does leadership responsibility equate to authority?
- If designated leaders do not have authority, then who does?
- How do different leadership roles relate to each other in the area of authority?

These are complicated questions. Wrong answers or confusing ones create chaos in churches. In fact, pastors, staff, and lay leaders of churches in virtually every community struggle with these issues.

So let's try to bring some order to the confusion. Our primary guide will be the Scriptures. I hope to help churches be able to better define the job descriptions of the various necessary leadership roles within their congregations. In this and the next two chapters we will address the job descriptions of elders, deacons, pastors, staff, and the laity.

I realize that churches differ in their polity as well as their terminology for church leadership. I am using the term *elder* to refer to what the Bible calls the *episkopos* in the Greek language. This is the office for which the qualifications are described by Paul in 1 Timothy 3:1–7 and Titus 1:5–9. Other English translations often used include the terms *overseer* or *bishop* for this role.

I am using the word *deacon,* which transliterates the Greek term *diakonos,* to describe a special servant-leadership role whose qualifications are described in 1 Timothy 3:8–13.

Because the emphasis in this chapter is on biblically based job descriptions, I encourage leaders in churches that do not use biblical terminology in their local church job descriptions to rethink their reasoning carefully. A church structure that includes only two categories (pastor and layperson) leaves out too much clear biblical teaching. A church structure that strictly assigns all the biblical terms (elder, deacon, bishop, pastor, evangelist) to professional staff runs the danger of disenfranchising much of the body of Christ. The biblical guidelines for job descriptions include some flexibility, but one of the underlying principles should be the following: *A healthy local church structure will include roles that express each of the biblical leadership positions. These two are elders and deacons.*

DEACONS: SERVICE

We begin with a brief word about deacons. The specific responsibilities of deacons are not laid out in a prescriptive manner in Scripture. In other words, the deacons' serving role appears to be quite broad. However, the role is generally described in the historic record (Acts 6:1–6), when this office was instituted. On that specific occasion, deacons were appointed to serve food daily to widows. That original involvement of deacons, however, does not determine the specific job description for deacons today. The central insight given into the role of the deacon is found in verses 2–4 of the passage. Deacons do that which frees the elders to do their job.

Thus, it appears that the job description of the deacon is to be shaped by the needs of the elders. We assume that, as illustrated in the early church, the focus of deacons will be directed to those with special needs within the church. Just as needs vary from community to community, time to time, and church to church, so we expect that the specifics of the deacons' job description will remain flexible.

Over and over I observe churches whose leadership is plagued with emotional conflict between an elder board and a deacon board. Clearly, both groups are biblically validated, but their working relationship within Scripture requires more attention. Deacons can feel somewhat insignificant in relation to elders. Confusion frequently exists, for example, over who has responsibility for the budget and finances of the church. Does money management fit the "holy" stereotype of the elder board or the "practical" stereotype of the deacon board? Many describe the role of deacon as minor-league duty before being called up to the major leagues, where the elders function.

The truth is that the position of deacon is not one of spiritual authority but one of service. Deacons are appointed or called to specific and temporary duties. Deacons serve elders and serve on behalf of elders. Elders, who hold the "keys" to God's kingdom (see below), do carry authority, yet they are charged to exercise it with a servant's heart. Deacons serve in a place of high honor. The first martyr in the Christian church was a deacon. The descriptions of Stephen's courage, faith, and witness in Acts chapters 6 and 7 refute any nonsense thinking about the role of deacon being minor league.

> THE DESCRIPTIONS OF STEPHEN'S COURAGE, FAITH, AND WITNESS . . . REFUTE ANY NONSENSE THINKING ABOUT THE ROLE OF DEACON BEING MINOR LEAGUE.

Regarding who has final responsibility over the budget and finances, go back to our earlier discussion on values. Who sets the values of the church? I suggest that this is the responsibility of the elders, who comprise the spiritual authority of the church. Now, if the highest spiritual authority in the local church does not also have final authority over finances, a contest of power invariably follows. Imagine what would happen in a church where the elders defined the value of outreach but the deacons determined the budget. Suppose the deacons allotted no money in the budget for outreach. Let me ask you, which group in reality has established the values? Obviously, the deacons. This does not mean that deacons have no say in establishing values or budget. A wise elder board seeks input from many sources. The issue is that the Scriptures entrust the final exercise of authority in the church not to an individual (such as a senior pastor) or any group that grasps power, but to a specific group representing the congregation called to wisely and prayerfully direct the church.

My continual counsel to the leadership of new church plants is to never allow the deacons to assume such responsibility. Let their role regarding finances be to distribute the monies to the needy as allotted by the elders of the church. I find that deacons who are truly called of God to their roles are excited to get out of administrative responsibilities in order to devote themselves to hands-on ministry to those in need. I would advise that as the church grows and the staff becomes capable of doing so, they be allowed to be involved in the spadework of budget preparation, leaving the responsibility of final approval to the elders.

ELDERS: GIVEN THE KEYS
OF THE KINGDOM OF HEAVEN

Let us now address the job description and role of the elder. Such a job description can never be clear without a biblical understanding of the authority vested in this office. To gain such an understanding, we once again turn to the passage discussed in chapter 1, Matthew 16:13–19. However, this time we are going to focus on what we can learn about the role of the elder.

After asking the Twelve about the public's opinions concerning Him, Jesus asked His disciples who they thought He was. Peter, speaking for the apostolic band, replied, "You are the Christ, the Son of the living God" (Matthew 16:16 NIV). To this confession Jesus responded, "You are Peter, and upon this rock I will build My church" (v. 18). Our Lord then made a declaration with far-reaching implications: "I will give you the keys of the kingdom of heaven; and whatever you shall bind on earth shall be bound in heaven, and whatever you loose on earth shall be loosed in heaven" (v. 19 NASB 1977).

What Are These Keys?

What are these "keys of the kingdom of heaven"? What are these "binding" and "loosing" functions of the keys? Keys have only two functions: to lock and to unlock. Possession of the keys represents authority to open and to shut. Since the new Israel of God, the church, is no longer a theocracy governed directly and immediately by God, God has determined that the church will function under His delegated authority—human leadership. Thus the "keys of the kingdom" represent the authority Christ has granted men to govern His church.

The church's leadership is granted specific authority "to bind" (to derive from God's Word and to enforce that which is obligatory) and "to loose" (to determine and allow that which the Word says is permissible). Spiritual authority thus discerns what is required and what is permitted. Why is this so important? Because the teaching of the Bible is often principle-focused rather than case-specific. Thus, wise judgments must be made in applying scriptural principles to particular situations. The "keys of the kingdom" are emblematic of the authority given to the church to determine the proper standards of biblical faith and practice and to carry out biblical discipline when required.

Who Holds the Keys?

So, we must answer the logical question: Specifically to whom in the church is this "binding and loosing" authority granted? Church history offers three predominant replies to this query.

As we noted earlier, during its foundational years the Roman Catholic Church adopted the view that the keys were given uniquely to Peter. According to this understanding, Peter alone received the keys and thus became the first pope, passing along the keys to generation after generation of popes throughout history.

But this interpretation appears to be based upon faulty exegesis. In the Greek language of the New Testament, the name Peter is *Petros,* meaning "small stone or pebble." But a different word, *petra,* meaning "a large boulder or underlying bedrock," is used in reference to the "rock" upon which Christ promised to build His church. Jesus thus employed a play on words in His reply to Peter, saying in effect, "Simon, you are Petros, a small pebble, solid but transitory. But it is upon the immovable bedrock of your confession that I am the Christ, the Son of the living God, that I will build My church." It was not Peter himself, but rather his confession of faith in Jesus that formed and maintains the foundation of the church.

Moreover, although the English *you* in "I will give you the keys," "whatever you bind," and "whatever you loose" is in its singular form in the Greek text of Matthew 16:13–19, the exact same teaching of Jesus in Matthew 18:18 uses the plural. The same truth is also conveyed in John 20:23 using the plural. In light of these other passages, it seems apparent that in Matthew 16, Jesus was speaking to Peter as representing the other apostles standing with him. Jesus indicated in His teaching that the proper recipients of the keys are several in number rather than being a single, particular person.

This observation leads to the second and third historic understandings of this passage. Both of these understandings rightly recognize the plurality of the key-holders. The distinction between the views lies in their differing identification of the key-holders.

The first of these last two views is represented by the practice of some modern churches that suggests that Jesus has given the keys of the kingdom to each individual believer. According to this view, when a believer exercises saving faith in Christ, he uses the keys to let himself into the kingdom. Churches adhering to this belief generally devalue the importance of church membership and may reject it altogether. If people believe they are Christians, they automatically think of themselves as being members of Christ's earthly church. Those holding this view often teach that membership in a local church is superfluous.

One difficulty with this position is that it makes each believer an authority unto himself and negates the need for church leadership and discipline. Advice, admonition, and rebuke offered by other, more mature believers have no more authority than any other opinion. This view also raises problems by its impracticality. What Christian who has fallen into habitual sin would use his set of keys to remove himself from church fellowship?

The last and most plausible of these views of the key-holders' identities has been adopted by the vast majority of Protestant churches throughout history. When He gave the keys of the kingdom, Jesus spoke not only to Peter but also to all the assembled apostles. He gave them collectively the authority to "bind and to loose," that is, to speak and to act for God. Jesus did not make them infallible (note Peter's repeated failures and denial). Nor did He make them sinless or perfect (note Judas's presence). This corporate apostolic authority was subsequently transferred through the laying on of hands to biblically qualified and selected elders in local churches

(1 Timothy 3:1–7; 4:14; Titus 1:5–9). The church has always been healthiest when she has lived under the leadership of wise elders functioning as a unit under the guidance of Scripture.

Such God-ordained elders continue to hold the keys of God's kingdom in the church today. It is their responsibility to protect the purity of the church and the honor of God's Word through biblical discipline of Christ's flock. They open church membership to professing believers, withhold membership from non-Christians, build up and encourage the repentant sinner, and dismiss the unrepentant from fellowship.

—॥॥—

THE PHRASE "CHURCH DISCIPLINE" HAS BECOME A SHOCKING OXYMORON.

—॥॥—

Again, as was true with the original disciples, the possession of the authority of the keys does not guarantee some sort of infallibility on the part of elders. Their decisions must be based on biblical grounds, and they do have boundaries. For instance, elders do not ultimately determine whether a particular person is or is not a Christian. Only God knows that with certainty. Nevertheless, the decisions and declarations of the elders carry the authority of God in such a way as to determine whether or not a person is to be treated as a Christian. It is in this context of understanding that the full meaning of passages such as Matthew 18:15–18 and Hebrews 13:17 is revealed:

> *"If your brother sins, go and reprove him in private; if he listens to you, you have won your brother. But if he does not listen to you, take one or two more with you, so that 'by the mouth of two or three witnesses every fact may be confirmed.' And if he refuses to listen to them, tell it to the church; and if he refuses to listen even to the church, let him be to you as a Gentile and a tax-gatherer. Truly I [Jesus] say to you, whatever you shall bind on earth shall be bound in heaven; and whatever you loose on earth shall be loosed in heaven."*
> —Matthew 18:15–18 NASB 1977

> *Obey your leaders and submit to them, for they keep watch over your souls as those who will give an account. Let them do this with joy and not with grief, for this would be unprofitable for you.*
> —Hebrews 13:17

In the passage from Matthew, "Let him be to you as a Gentile and a tax-gatherer" means, "Let him be treated as a nonbeliever," which in practice means removing a person from church membership. "Leaders" in Hebrews 13 refers to those ordained as elders in the church, who plainly have the authority and the responsibility to faithfully direct God's church.

The Will and the Wisdom of God

In these Scripture passages and others, the Lord has indicated the nature of the authority He wishes to be exercised in His church. Other passages speak of the authority God intends to be exercised in the other two of the three foundational institutions He has ordained for the benefit of society: the state and the family (see Romans 13:1–7; Ephesians 5:22–6:4). A specific leadership authority has been granted the right and the responsibility to bless the good and discipline the wicked in each of three areas:

- Parents in the family
- Civil magistrates and governors in the state
- Elders in the church

For the most part, members of society obey the laws of the state, if for no other reason than to avoid the civil and criminal penalties of lawbreaking. The authority of parents appears to have been in decline over the years, as the practice of loving but firm corrective discipline has been widely abandoned. The authority of the church was disregarded long ago, in part because of faulty interpretations of the passages cited above and in part because of the unwillingness of the church to enforce biblical discipline even when such a responsibility is recognized and badly needed.

Unfortunately, clear biblical teaching on this subject is almost extinct today. It is so foreign, in fact, that you may still be scratching your head. The phrase "church discipline" has become a shocking oxymoron. For this reason, perhaps I should address an important issue to further enable you to understand the authority given to elders. There is a distinction, I believe, between what I call the authority to determine the will of God and the authority to determine the wisdom of God. The point is that unless they contradict the infallible Word of God, elders' decisions regarding moral and ecclesiastical matters always declare the will of God even though they often fail to declare the wisdom of God. Allow me to illustrate.

We have already pointed out that parents have been given authority from God over their children (Ephesians 6:1). Likewise, the civil magistrate (government) has been given authority over its citizens and residents (Romans 13:1–2). With this in mind, how would you answer the following question? If a child chooses not to obey her parents, even though their orders do not contradict God's Word, has she violated the will of God? Of course she has. She may argue, "Show me in the Bible where it says to be home at ten o'clock at night and I'll do it, because I certainly want to obey God. I don't think it's God's will for you to arbitrarily set my curfew time."

If this were your child, your response would more than likely be, "What I say is God's will for you because I am your parent." But what if you gave in to her desires and told her to be home at two o'clock in the morning? If she came in at ten till two, would she be "in the will of God"? I say yes. In this case, you, as the parent, have declared for your daughter what is the will of God. In my opinion, however, you have failed to declare the wisdom of God. Establishing a curfew is your authority responsibility; establishing a right and healthy curfew is your godly wisdom responsibility.

For an interesting study on the contrast between the will of God and the wisdom of God exercised in a home, read the account of Nabal, Abigail, and David in 1 Samuel 25:2–38. Nabal's authority in his home was honored (God's will) even though Nabal exercised that authority stupidly (not God's wisdom).

The same holds true for God's other institutions, the civil magistrate and the church. When our church decided several years ago to relocate, I often heard the question, "Are we sure this is the will of God?" I was glad to know that such was the heart and concern of our people. At a meeting to update the people concerning the progress of the effort, I addressed this matter. My comments went something like this:

> In response to the often-asked question, "Is this relocation the will of God?" I have some very important news. Without any question whatsoever, God has made it known with perfect clarity that it is His will for us to attempt the relocation.

I could sense the thoughts of our people as I said this. *Man, this doesn't sound like Randy. In what ivory tower has he been meeting with God?* So I concluded by saying:

I can say so with such absolute confidence because our elders voted to do so. They have prayerfully exercised their authority responsibility. Now, although I know it's God's will to pursue the relocation, I have no such certainty that the decision reflects the wisdom of God. Only time will tell.

We apply this principle in other settings. When two members of our church have a financial dispute in a business matter and follow Paul's instructions to the church at Corinth to take the issue to the church rather than the courts, we see the value of this teaching. After argument is made from both sides, the elders have to make a decision. Whatever that decision is, the party ruled against must see that "whatever you [the elders] shall bind on earth shall be bound in heaven" (Matthew 16:19 NASB 1977). Thus, the decision made on earth (assuming it doesn't contradict the Word of God) becomes that upon which the Lord places His approval. This is to carry the authority of His will. In many of the same decisions, I'm sure eternity will reveal much lack of wisdom, even some mistakes. Nevertheless, even as in a civil court of law, the authority rests in those holding the responsibility to make the decision.

Similarly, the real test of a child's obedience and honor toward his or her parents doesn't involve obeying just the wise and thoughtful rules but also the fickle and unwise ones. In Luke 2, Jesus was content remaining "in My Father's house" (v. 49) while Mary and Joseph searched for him frantically. But when they insisted He return to Nazareth with them, He went willingly. That's the point at which Luke declares, "And Jesus grew in wisdom and stature, and in favor with God and men" (v. 52 NIV). The test of submission to authority doesn't come when that authority tells us we can do what we want but when that authority blocks our will or reaches a conclusion we are sure is wrong.

I have emphasized this point regarding the authority vested in elders for two reasons: (1) to stress the importance of wise submission by those under authority, and (2) to impress upon us the sober responsibility God has given to those who hold this office. Their declarations express God's will. That role should never be taken lightly or proudly. Elders must humbly ensure that their primary responsibility never gets lost behind lesser duties, such as directing programs and attending monthly meetings.

Key Tasks of Leadership

Those who are elders have been called to "shepherd the flock of God" (1 Peter 5:2). They are described as those who "watch over your souls as those who will give an account" (Hebrews 13:17). Since such responsibilities are made so clear in Scripture, allow me to suggest that those who hold the keys to the kingdom must give themselves primarily to pastoring, leading, teaching, and discipling. Such roles can be performed in a variety of different manners, but should never be allowed to degenerate to merely administrative functions.

STAFF VERSUS ELDERS

Of all the organizational dilemmas that have challenged Perimeter Church, perhaps the most significant has been trying to determine how to maintain the line of distinction between the responsibilities and authority of the staff and those of the elders.

When our church was only a couple of years old, one of our elders spoke with great emotion during one of our meetings regarding a concern he had. A church member had asked him a question regarding a program in our church about which he was unaware. He said passionately that something was wrong when an elder was so uninformed. At this point, another elder, who was seasoned and grayed enough to really look the part, challenged all of us elders to rethink our role in decision making. He suggested that regarding decision making, the elders should deal only with policy and leave the programming decisions to me in my specific duties as pastor, to our staff, and to the many ministry team lay leaders. Seizing on the fact that most of the elders were businessmen, he asked how many of the companies for which they worked operated with the board of directors making the day-to-day operational decisions. We decided then that the staff would be responsible for programming and the elders would take care of policy making, discipline and theological issues, staff personnel issues, and approval of our overall ministry plan.

But how easily all this was forgotten. Within a few years, our elder ministry team was composed of totally different people. Standards of operation had not yet been written. We weren't very consistent in our elder orientation, and those who had joined us from different church backgrounds held different assumptions. I had fallen into the mistaken habit of bringing major program decisions to the elder team. Most of these issues were ones the staff had already debated for hours. When the elders tried to debate the same issues in the half hour allotted for discussion, faulty decisions resulted.

On one occasion, seeing where the discussion was headed, I observed that our staff had already been down that road only to find a dead end. With that, one of the elders spoke up in frustration and said, "If you want us just to rubber-stamp the staff's decisions, then we don't need to be here. Either you guys make these decisions or allow us to labor long enough on these issues to draw our own conclusions."

I called church expert Lyle Schaller for some outside counsel. I told him of my frustration and asked him to what degree elders should be involved in making program decisions. His response was that the only lay elders who should be participating in approving or disapproving programs were those who volunteered on the average of fifty hours a week. I think he was perhaps intentionally overstating the case to make his point. But his rationale was that it takes full-time involvement in the overall life of the church to understand the implications of one program on the whole of the ministry. Only broad experience allows a leader to see how approval of one ministry may well take the resources away from another.

Though the elders no longer spend time making decisions about programs, I do go to them from time to time for counsel about programming issues that may impact our vision or mission. I value their wise perspective on major decisions. Our elders are pleased that they can give their time primarily to matters such as pastoring me, holding me accountable in my spiritual pilgrimage, laying hands on me and praying over me for lengthy periods of time each month, and dealing with the policy and personnel issues of our church. We now take more care and time with the orientation and training of new elders. Many of the principles we have developed for discipleship have specific application in the preparation of elders for their unique leadership ministry.

THE SIZE OF AN ELDER BOARD

The question regarding the size of an elder team or board must be addressed. There are no numerical biblical directives to be heeded. Because I believe that an elder's job is permanent until he surrenders his ordination for some reason or needs to be dismissed, and because we can never have too many pastors, teachers, and disciplers, we elect and ordain as many who are qualified and willing to serve. From this pool of elders, three are appointed each year to join a team of six other elders to serve for three years, giving leadership to the church by serving on what we call the Elder Ministry Team (EMT). We have nine ruling elders on our EMT.

Although those elders and I have an equal vote on any issue, in reality ten elders is probably too many for this highly specialized role. Schaller argues for boards of either five or seven. We have chosen a larger size due to travel schedules and periodic transfers. Also, our elder team divides into two work teams each month to prepare for our monthly elders' meeting. That makes each committee just the right size. So ten seems to work well for us. By the way, we also find it helpful to include in each yearly class two elders who are relatively new to our church so that we don't find ourselves always thinking in the past. At the same time, we like one of three elders per year to have previously served to make sure we maintain continuity with our past.

The choice of these three men each year is as critical as the annual election of new elders. Let me suggest that you require your leadership not only to meet the character standards described in Timothy and Titus but also to study your ministry plan adequately and commit full support to it. These leaders form the backbone of the congregation, and they provide the supporting supervision for the specialized roles we will examine in the next chapter.

Note

1. Robert H. Schuller, *Your Church Has Real Possibilities* (Glendale, Calif.: Regal, 1974), 49.

11

BIBLICALLY BASED JOB DESCRIPTIONS— THE ROLE OF THE PASTOR

The authority of elders and the serving roles of deacons, noted in chapter 10, comprise the general leadership roles within the church. The specialized roles of pastor and laity are the focus of this and the next chapter. *Pastor* and *laity* are terms used more often than they are clearly understood. And though their definitions may vary among churches, the emphasis here has to do with maintaining the clarity and purpose of each role.

Scripture uses the title "pastor-teacher" to refer to those gifted to shepherd God's people with a primary emphasis on teaching. This person is admonished in Scripture to "equip the saints for the work of ministry" (Ephesians 4:12 NRSV). With this responsibility in mind, I like to refer to the pastor as a *leader-equipper*. If the health of the local church (as we have seen) is going to be measured by the degree to which believers become mature and equipped followers of

Jesus Christ, then someone has to be responsible to ensure that the objective is accomplished—equipping and leading them.

EQUIPPING: THREE VIEWS

The Traditional View

There are three views of the pastor's role of equipping those within the church. The *traditional view* sees the role of the pastor and staff as paid professionals who do whatever jobs are needed. If the church needs teaching, hire a teacher. If the church needs evangelism to be accomplished, hire an evangelist. And if the church needs pastoring, hire a pastor. Unfortunately, we are all too familiar with this less-than-biblical, pastor-as-hired-gun perspective.

The Evangelical View

The *evangelical view* sees the role of the pastor and staff as first, to help the church members discover their spiritual gifts (special abilities given by God's grace to enhance the work of God's kingdom); and second, to start needed ministries within the church and community. Then, last, the pastor is to recruit the appropriately gifted people to the appropriate ministry.

The evangelical view sounds pretty good, doesn't it? Not from my perspective! Most who have actually tried to put this view into practice agree with me. This approach reminds me of the circus act where the performer comes out with a stack of plates and begins spinning them on sticks stationed on the floor. By the time the tenth plate is up and spinning, the first is beginning to wobble. The performer races back to the first and revs up every stick until all are safely in motion again, allowing him to set plates eleven through twenty spinning. From that point on he frantically runs from plate to plate giving each stick just enough attention to keep the whole precarious arrangement spinning. So goes the life of a pastor who lives out this second approach. A vacation could be disastrous.

Years ago a couple moved to Atlanta and began attending our church. He had been a successful pastor, and she had experienced a full life as the first lady of their church. He had now taken a position with a parachurch organization in Atlanta. The wife was an attractive and very gifted woman—as well equipped for ministry as any woman in our congregation at that time. I assumed they were happy campers in our church until the day I got a stinging letter from her, filled with expressions of hurt, disappointment, and anger. She explained that the past two years of her life in Atlanta had been the first in her adult life that she had no ministry. She went on to reveal the cause of her plight by pointing a finger at me. According to her, I was guilty of gross negligence because I, as the senior pastor, had never personally given her a ministry. She apparently embraced this "evangelical view" of equipping, and I had offended and disappointed her. She had waited two years for the "spin" that never came. As a result, she explained, she and her husband had decided to leave our church.

I wrote her a gracious letter (as I do to all people who choose to express directly to me their disappointment with me or with the church). Since she had mentioned in her letter the church they would begin attending, I asked her to do herself and her new pastor (a personal friend of mine) a favor—to realize that she didn't need her pastor's permission to do ministry. God had already given it. I encouraged her to go to her pastor if she needed equipping or help in doing ministry, but never to think that God must speak through her pastor in order to legitimize her ministry.

The Biblical View

This leads us to the third view. The last approach to pastoral ministry I call the *biblical view* of equipping. Those who hold this perspective believe that the pastor and staff's responsibility is to help the church's members discover their spiritual gifts, but then to simply create an environment where God's voice can be heard. Since we embrace this view, we encourage the people of Perimeter to seek God for His leading in ministry and then, if they need help discerning that leading or need equipping to perform that ministry, to call upon us.

The Greek word translated "to equip" is *katartizo* and carries the idea of coming alongside as one seeks to arrive at his destiny—not to pull "sitters" off the bench. The perspective that members have regarding equipping will dictate their expectations and shape their involvement in the church. Only God knows accurately what ministry is best for each of His children.

WHO DOES WHAT?

Many of you reading this book probably know more about business than you do about church organization. So allow me to illustrate from your world. A business always knows who its customers, employees, and employers are. But I believe most church members don't know who takes these roles in the church. Do you? I ask this question of each monthly Inquirer's Class, which spends a weekend investigating the life of our church. When I ask who the church's customer is, I repeatedly hear a variety of answers—nonmembers, seekers, other believers—and a lot of uncertainty even in those whose responses are accurate. Then I suggest that, since we don't have agreement, we move along to the role of employee.

When I ask who they think serves in the church in a role comparable to the employee within a business, you could guess the answers. Some would say, staff members; others, church members; and others, ordained pastors. Only when I ask whom they see functioning in the role of employer do I get unanimity in response. Everyone agrees that God is the employer—until I ask them who the owner is. Of course, I explain that within a business you may well have an owner and employer being the same person, so technically they are right. But, assuming a four-tier organization as listed below, I ask them to begin at the top with God as the owner and to work down, seeking to determine who fulfills the roles of the other three, to "fill in the blanks."

Owner	=	God
Employer	=	_____
Employee	=	_____
Customer	=	_____

At this point people usually agree that the staff (after I explain that they serve with the elders and under their authority) serve in the role of employer. The members of the church, they agree, occupy the role of employee. Then, when all agree that the unchurched are our customers, I explain that church members are also our customers because we are also called to minister to one another.

Now, look at the filled-in blanks below and answer the question, Whose responsibility is it to reach the customer? The answer, *employee*, becomes obvious. So what is the role of the employer? The answer: to invest in the employee in such a way as to enable that person to do his or her job adequately. This involves leading and equipping, among other things.

Owner	=	God
Employer	=	Elders/Staff
Employee	=	Members
Customer	=	Unchurched and Members

The Scriptures tell us that the same is true in the life of God's church. Ephesians 4:11–12 explains that pastor-teachers are to equip the saints for the work of ministry. Judged by the actual practice in most churches, you would think that God gave pastor-teachers to do the work of ministry. To the degree that equipping remains an optional duty and the saints become an insignificant middleman in God's design for ministry, the church will not prevail.

Keeping our business illustration in mind, imagine that I am the regional sales manager of a large company. I have just gathered my sales force for quarterly sales reports. I begin, in roll-call fashion, to call out names. "Jo Anne?"

Jo Anne responds simply, "No sales to report."

Shocked, to say the least, I show restraint and say nothing, simply moving to the next name. "John?"

As before, the response is simply, "No sales to report." Now I am flabbergasted. This is, after all, a sales report meeting! After hearing the next five employees give the same response, I look out over the audience of salesmen and women and ask, with great frustration, "Who has had any sales? Raise your hands." Not one hand goes up. Then I go ballistic and begin railing at my sales force for their laziness and irresponsibility.

In the midst of this, Scott stands up and speaks for the rest of the team. He says, "Randy, don't be so alarmed. We want you to know that we have all worked very diligently this past quarter."

> IN MUCH OF THE CHURCH TODAY, MEMBERS ARE SPENDING MUCH OF THEIR TIME WORKING TO ENHANCE THEIR OWN EMPLOYEE BENEFITS AND FAILING TO GIVE THEMSELVES TO . . . REACHING THE CUSTOMER.

I interrupt, concerned. "Oh no, I can't believe it! Our competition must have overtaken us. They've bettered our product."

Scott speaks up again and says, "No, we still have the best product in the market."

More confused, I blurt out, "Oh no, my worst fear! There's no longer a market for our product."

Again, Scott corrects me by saying, "Randy, relax. Wrong again. We have worked hard. The market is wide-open and we have the best product at the lowest price."

"I surrender," I say, and throw up my hands. "Help me out. I don't understand."

"Randy, we have been working hard this quarter," Scott replies, "but what we've been doing is spending our time trying to come up with new and improved employee benefit plans. We've got some great ideas to suggest to you and then the management. Aren't you excited, Randy?"

"Not in the least!" I answer, practically screaming. "That's not your job."

In much of the church today, members are spending much of their time working to enhance their own employee benefits and failing to give themselves to the task of reaching the customer. This is one of the main reasons for the ineffectiveness of the church. Having read the scenario above, you might expect me to rail against lax church members. What I am going to do, however, is to address the pastor's leadership job description. Notice that I say leadership job description, not pastoral job description (which will be discussed later).

THE ROLE OF THE SENIOR PASTOR

I believe that the pastor's leadership job description should include four primary responsibilities.

1. Spend time with God to discern His leading for the church.

The pastor is to spend time with the Lord discerning His leading regarding the future direction of the church. Quite a while ago, I read that the president of an Ivy League school said something like this: "Unless 20 percent of my time is spent with my feet on my desk, I can only manage this organization—but I cannot lead it."

He was saying that he had to spend time away from the day-to-day responsibilities that robbed him of the time to think about the future.

In the early years of our church, the elders told me they wanted me to spend four weeks a year away from my regular responsibilities to spend time talking and listening to God, thinking ahead, planning for the future, and sharing this direction with our leadership. I have kept this practice now for nearly twenty-five years and have never regretted the time spent away.

2. Set goals for the church.

The leader-equipper sets goals for the church according to the will of God. In our church polity, the elders ultimately approve our goals, but they rely on me and our staff to wrestle with the initial formation of those goals and then to make recommendations.

3. Share the vision and goals with the people.

The leader-equipper shares vision and goals with the people, seeking their enthusiasm and ownership. If the members do not understand or accept their role in the church, the system will break down. This is one of the most difficult assignments to accomplish in any church—especially in a large church. Finding the appropriate time and place is the issue. Doubtlessly, the most significant time to do this, for us, has been a special series of banquets offered prior to the beginning of our new ministry year. Everyone is urged to attend one of these banquets where, in addition to outstanding food, music, and drama, I share the vision and goals for the coming year of ministry. Obviously vision is cast in many different venues, but this has proven to be our most effective setting.

4. See that each church member is equipped to help in accomplishing these goals.

Finally, the leader-equipper sees that each member of the church is properly equipped to do his or her part in accomplishing these goals. We will say more about this in chapter 13, which discusses strategically designed infrastructure.

WHAT ABOUT PASTORAL RESPONSIBILITIES?

So much for the pastor's leadership job description. What about his *pastoral* job description? What should the pastor's shepherding responsibilities be?

Consider an imaginary church of at least a hundred members. One hundred members can actually represent hundreds of people whose problems could ultimately necessitate the time of the pastor. For instance, if a member's parent in another state is diagnosed with cancer, the member now has a problem. If a member's next-door neighbor is depressed and needs pastoral help or is going through a divorce and needs counsel, the pastor is most likely to be asked to respond. All of a sudden, this church of one hundred members represents hundreds of people who may need the pastor on any given day. And the larger the church, the more accentuated the problem.

Pastors' days can generally be divided into three major responsibilities (shown above): meeting pastoral responsibilities (P), leading and equipping (L with dotted E), and personal time (the smaller circle in each illustration)—family time, time for personal worship, leisure, physical exercise, sleep. Each circle represents a different way pastors can handle these three duties. In circle one, the pastor spends most of the time responding to pastoral needs. In the second circle, the personal life gets pushed aside. Too often this happens, as the pastor's entire life is filled with church, both pastoring and leading and equipping. I am amazed how many pastors lose their kids as a result of the failure to spend adequate time with them. It's also common to find pastors out of physical condition and spending little time in personal worship. And to make it worse, these imbalances are often excused and praised as evidence of hard work and faithfulness to the call of God.

The goal is the balanced life, shown in the third large circle—with pastoral responsibilities no longer competing with leading and equipping duties, and personal activities included in the schedule.

Please don't misinterpret my next comments about the time constraints pastors face. Those in my profession have no corner of ownership on time pressure and fatigue. Pastors for the most part don't work longer hours than many other professionals. But pastors do work different hours than those in the marketplace (which is neither better nor worse). Many laypeople have to leave for work five days a week at six o'clock in the morning and don't return home until seven in the evening. Yet I can manage my schedule so as to take off work in the midafternoon, if I choose.

I have often been the only male parent at a child's ball practice. What an advantage! On the other hand, it is not unusual for me to work thirty of my weekly hours outside the traditional work times of eight to five, Monday through Friday. Much of my work has to be done in early morning and night meetings and weekend activities. The issue is not one of when does one work, but of whether or not one's work robs a person of his or her higher priorities.

It has not been uncommon through the years for one of my children to ask me in the morning whether I would be home that night. More often than not my response has been, "No." However, I have also been able to say, "But I will be home at three this afternoon and will play with you till dinnertime."

On many occasions, immediately prior to this important hour, as I'm packing up to leave the office, my secretary will hand me a few "important" phone messages. Now I have church members who expect me to call immediately, but I also have a child who needs me at home. What do I do? Unfortunately, too often in the early years of ministry, I would reluctantly go to the phone and return those calls—and far too often have to return home later than scheduled only to seek forgiveness from my child.

Do you know why I made such unwise choices? Because I am insecure. I love the approval of my peers. My reasoning at the time was, I know these people. God calls them His sheep and they are, but I have learned all too well that sheep bite tenaciously. On the other hand, my child is so gracious, and I know he or she will understand. Here's the danger, however. Though the child may be sweet now, he may express his displeasure in profound ways at age sixteen or seventeen. A little child may repeatedly understand

and forgive a parent's insensitivity and inconsistencies, but a child will not know what to do with the hurt that remains even after forgiveness. If that hurt accumulates enough, it will eventually spill over into shocking results.

Through the years I have learned that the same sheep who would bite me if I didn't meet their need upon request are the very ones who would say, if my child rebelled, "If anyone should model the family, it's the pastor. He should have spent more time with his children." The way I look at it, if I'm going to be criticized one way or the other, why not do so while keeping my kids on my team?

So what should the pastor's pastoral responsibilities be? I suggest four primary commitments:

1. Shepherd the staff
2. Shepherd the elders
3. Shepherd personal friends in crisis
4. Shepherd every person in need who makes their needs known when no one else is equipped yet to minister to them

Notice that the solution never involves allowing people's genuine needs to go unmet so that the pastor can maintain attention to his own well-being. If I, as a pastor, have not equipped anyone to meet a particular person's needs, then it becomes my job. The greater the number of needs or roles in the church that only the pastor can meet, the more evidence exists that the pastor is failing to equip enough people to do the work of the ministry.

THE COST OF EFFECTIVENESS

Effective ministry—ministry that helps to grow the church as Jesus commanded—pays a price. Pastors and other staff leadership must be willing to (1) assume responsibility for failure, (2) major on their primary responsibilities, and (3) share ministry responsibility with the laity.

1. Assume responsibility for failure.

All of us who are pastors are guilty at one time or another of complaining about our jobs. Surely, many of those complaints are well-founded. But one does not stand up to scrutiny. It is the complaint of having bad, unleadable, unwilling-to-serve laity. Certainly every church does have its few, but for the most part, church members go where they are led. They grow up as strong as the environment in which they are placed.

My undergraduate work was at the University of Alabama during the days of Alabama football coach Paul "Bear" Bryant. I was an ardent student of him as a leader. Rarely have I observed anyone with greater strength in leadership abilities, and his understanding of leadership seemed to match his abilities.

On one occasion near the end of his extremely successful career, he read in the *Atlanta Journal-Constitution* a quote from the Georgia Tech football coach, Bill Curry. Curry was in the midst of a terrible season and had lost the game on the previous day. He was interviewed by the media, and he refused to take responsibility for the loss. He explained that he had taken responsibility for losing all year but not now. His explanation was that he and his coaches had done their jobs and that on this particular week the players just didn't have the heart and will to win.

During a speech after this episode, Bill Curry revealed he answered a phone call on that following Monday morning from Bear Bryant. Coach Bryant talked to Curry as a coach would talk to an inattentive player or a father would address his son. He said, "Bill, I read your statement after Saturday's game about not taking responsibility for this loss. I don't ever want to hear such a comment from you ever again. Never forget, you are the leader. You recruited these players. You coach these players. You are the one who must motivate these players. When you lose, you take responsibility for the loss. And, oh, by the way, when you win, you give the boys the credit."

Good leaders take responsibility for the failure of the organization they lead.

2. Major on their primary responsibilities.

Pastoral and staff leadership must pay the cost of sticking to that which God has called them to, regardless of others' expectations. They must be willing to focus on their primary responsibilities.

3. Share ministry responsibility with the laity.

Many pastors do not want to share the pastoral responsibilities because nothing invites the accolades and approval of members like pastoring them in their time of need. Do so and they will support you and love you for the rest of your ministry. On the other hand, equip people to do the ministry and you may not get even as much as a "thank-you" from those whose needs have been met.

Yes, the cost of sticking to your job duties is high, but so are the benefits. A healthy and humbling satisfaction occurs when someone you have equipped is highly praised for his or her ministry. God's kingdom is richly blessed, and thus the King of the kingdom is honored.

12

BIBLICALLY BASED JOB DESCRIPTIONS— THE ROLE OF THE LAITY

The expression "Every member a minister" has gained wide popularity among churches. We use it frequently at Perimeter. But we have also been reminded that a description is less than an accomplishment. Many churches that print the claim "Every member a minister" on their weekly bulletin would be hard-pressed to describe what that phrase actually means. The first Reformation gave the Word of God back to the people of God. Today we need a second Reformation that gives the work of God back to the people of God. That will not happen until the laity accept their role as ministers.

The only way the pastor and staff of a church can fulfill their rightful job descriptions is for the laity to fulfill theirs. The roles are inseparable and interdependent. Like two sides of a coin, one cannot exist without the other.

WHAT SHOULD A LAYPERSON DO?

Four primary responsibilities ought to be included in a biblically oriented job description for the laypeople in the church:

1. *To discover and develop their spiritual gifts.* Every church ought to have a vehicle to systematically introduce believers to the teaching of God's Word regarding spiritual gifts. The availability of these tools has greatly enhanced the possibility of equipping, but not if they are left unused.
2. *To view themselves as the primary ministers of the church.* This description is almost as easy to say as "Every member a minister." The truth is that the laity will not see themselves in this way until the leadership in the church persistently sees them that way. The laity should be considered the primary ministers of the church and must be willing to deliberately lay claim to that role.
3. *To spend the time needed to be equipped adequately to use their spiritual gifts.* Gifts take time to develop. Much effort must be invested in learning to steward these gifts well so as to maximize one's impact with their usage.
4. *To commit the time necessary to use their gifts in ministry.* To have the necessary gifts and even to be proficient in their usage is of no value if there is no time available to put them to use. Time must be scheduled for such.

Let's look in detail at the second great responsibility of the laity, to view themselves as the primary ministers of the church. How can this transition take place? Perhaps Joe's story will illustrate best.

JOE'S STORY

Joe and his family had moved to Atlanta from Alabama. Joe and Catherine had three children, a daughter in high school and two junior-high-age sons. Because this family had been active members of a Protestant church, Joe assumed he was a believer. But constant exposure to God's Word and God's people revealed to him otherwise. By the age of forty, Joe was already a successful businessman. Both his feet were firmly planted in the middle of the world's values.

But when he met Christ in a life-transforming way, everything he stood for began to change. In a sense, he took a step into the kingdom of God and his weight shifted irreversibly toward eternity. One foot, however, was still stuck in his previous way of living. During that time period, Joe could have easily been compared to the Corinthians addressed by Paul in 1 Corinthians 3. He was still "fleshly . . . walking like mere men" (v. 3). Joe's new life was under construction, but not without the trials and problems God often uses as the instruments of purging.

Meanwhile, Joe's daughter, Jessica, graduated from high school. She had been not only a spiritual leader but also quite popular. She was selected to be both a cheerleader and the homecoming queen, all the while maintaining a reputation as a young person who took God seriously. When she graduated from high school, she went on to the University of Alabama.

Only a few weeks into her freshman year, Jessica was killed in a car wreck. As could be imagined, Joe's heart was pierced through and through. In the midst of the pain of this human tragedy, Joe sensed his dragging foot, previously caught in the attachments of this world, begin to loosen. After all, a big part of his reason for interest in this world was now in the next— and his heart followed.

Soon after Jessica's tragic death, Joe found out he had inoperable and terminal cancer. He underwent chemotherapy treatment, but the powerful drugs were only able to slow down the disease. Faced with the reality of a shortened life expectancy (outside a supernatural healing of God), Joe's back foot, until then caught up in the world's priorities, lifted and swung freely into the realm of eternal pursuit. After all, what did the world have to offer him now? (By the way, how often do you think about the fact that we are all dying right now and that everyone we love will also die one day? Why do we keep senselessly investing in the things of this world?)

> WE NEED TO GIVE THE WORK OF GOD BACK TO THE PEOPLE OF GOD.

Even as his body deteriorated, Joe experienced accelerated spiritual growth. His past lifestyle, by choice and by doctor's orders, changed radically. He had to cease the day-to-day responsibilities of his occupation. His fast-paced life shifted into low gear. Suddenly, Joe had a lot of immediate time on his hands and little reason to worry about long-term plans. At this point he was still mobile, driving his car and doing basic daily functions and caring for his family.

Pause

Let's put the story of Joe on pause for a moment. From time to time, especially in the early years of our church, I received calls from pastors of churches outside of Atlanta telling me of members of their churches who were in Atlanta receiving special medical treatment at Emory Hospital. These pastors would ask if I could be their members' pastor while they were in Atlanta, visiting them and ministering to them as often as possible. These pastors were unaware that such a visit from where I live would take the better part of a half day. Unable to meet this need personally, I nevertheless always responded by saying, "I can't promise you that I will minister to them, but I can assure you that I'll have someone who is adequately equipped do so."

One pastor responded to this answer by saying, "Well, if it's not an ordained clergy, don't waste their time. My member will not accept the ministry of someone not ordained."

Can you believe it? Those church members don't even know me! That pastor greatly underestimated the power of peer ministry. Many of our laity are far more gifted and qualified to do pastoral care work than I am.

In fact, I freely admit that if someone needs pastoral care and gets me as their pastor, compared to these other more gifted laypeople, they get ripped off! Though I know I have the heart of a pastor, I don't have many of the gifts related to crisis pastoral care. I don't hold hands well with people when they hurt. I don't cry well with those who cry. I could go on and on. God did not give me the gift of mercy. When I walk into a hospital room and see a tube in someone's throat, my first thought may well be one of empathy, but my first response might be to question whether the tube is really needed!

Many years ago, I used to visit every woman in our church who had a baby. Not only did this create much work for me, but very stressful work at that! I know this may sound odd to you, but figuratively speaking, I would drive around the hospital parking lot several times, mustering up the courage to perform my obligation. Perhaps you are thinking, *Grow up, Randy. How can you be hesitating over the easiest and most pleasant kind of hospital visit?*

But my response to those who would think this way is as follows.

How would you feel if someone gave you an assignment of having lunch with someone you have never met, with the specific purpose of sharing Christ with him? Assume that you are told that this person is intellectually more capable than you and, in fact, a near genius. You also discover that this person is rude and downright mean, expressing hatred toward Christians and always looking for a good debate to put down Christianity. I imagine that some of you reading this would perhaps, figuratively speaking, drive around the restaurant parking lot several times before going in—if you even went in at all. Do you know my first response to such avoidance? "Grow up." You see, God has made me in such a way that when I have that challenge facing me at the end of the week, I wake up each morning counting down the days to this upcoming highlight of my ministry week.

The point is that God has gifted us all differently, and we must respect and work according to these differences. What I see in church after church are multitudes of God's people with amazing gifts for ministry sitting idle while a handful of "professionals" try to do too much of what they are not particularly gifted to do. We need to give the work of God back to the people of God!

Back to Joe's Story

About this time in Joe's spiritual odyssey, I received a request to visit a man who was a patient at Emory, and I gave my typical response.

The relieved pastor said, "Fine. Thank you for any help you can offer."

I asked a little about his member's history and character, looking for some insight that might help me assign the right person to minister to him. When I was told that this man was dying of cancer and was taking chemotherapy, I immediately thought of Joe as my potential ministry candidate. I called Joe to ask if he could help me. He graciously volunteered to help in any way that he could. I explained to Joe that I needed him to go to Emory and be a minister to a man dying of cancer.

Joe's immediate response was to say that he would have no idea how to perform such a ministry. I explained that his lack of preparation was my fault because I am an equipper of the saints and I had failed to do my job! I asked if he would agree to do his job as a minister on the condition that I would first do mine as the equipper. He agreed.

After giving Joe some simple equipping and encouragement on what to do and how to perform his ministry, I sent him on his way to Emory. Later that day Joe rushed into my office and exclaimed, "Randy, you told me this man was dying, but you didn't tell me that he's probably going to die in the next few days and that he's not a believer! Randy, you've got to get to that hospital and witness to him before he dies."

I hope that by now my response won't surprise you. I said, "Joe, did you know you don't have to be ordained to share the gospel?"

He responded, "I have no idea how to share the gospel." I explained, once again, that that was my fault. I am an equipper and had failed to equip him for one of life's most important responsibilities as a believer. I asked if he would be willing to do his job on the condition that I would be willing to do my job. He reluctantly agreed.

After a crash course on sharing his faith, Joe made his way back to Emory. He shared the gospel with this man and visited him daily until the man died.

Now there's no story of salvation to report, but Joe's response was significant. Catching me outside the auditorium after a service, Joe said to me, "Randy, I've been thinking and have come to the conclusion that you should never go to hospitals to do pastoral work."

I asked him to explain.

He answered, "Be honest. How many times would you have visited this man with cancer? Once?"

I agreed.

He said, "That's all that could be expected of you. There's one of you and many sick people. But for me, no one expects me to do pastoral work at the hospital. So I can concentrate on one person and give him more attention than you could."

I agreed.

Then he added in his own humorous but sincere way, "And besides, I think I probably did a better job than you could have done!" I loved hearing this and was delighted by how this experience had impacted his life.

But this story has one more chapter. Not long after this episode, I got a call from Joe. I heard concern in his tone of voice and asked what the problem was. He explained that he had just received a phone call from his thirty-eight-year-old neighbor. This young man's wife had dropped dead, apparently of a heart attack, while in their kitchen cooking with her two young daughters. The shattered husband was in shock and uncertain what to do. He told Joe that just the week before he and his wife had been driving along talking about Jessica's funeral—how unique and celebratory it had been.

During that conversation they had also briefly discussed their own situation. Since neither of them had a church or a pastor, they wondered what they would do if something happened to one of them. The wife said to her husband, "If I die before you, I'd like for you to see if Joe's pastor is still in Atlanta. And if he is, I would like him to do my funeral." Little did either of them realize that this would be perhaps her final request. With those words in mind, this man had called Joe to ask him to call me to see if I would be his pastor during his time of need.

Joe said to me, "Randy, I know you can't do everyone's friend's funeral, but in light of the uniqueness of this situation, would you be willing to be this family's pastor?"

To this I responded, "Joe, did you know that you don't have to be ordained to do funerals?" Joe did everything but drop the phone. He knew what was coming. He said, "Oh no! Hospital visitation and witnessing, yes, but not funerals. No way."

My honest reply to Joe was that I could not do it but would consider it my job to equip him to meet that need. Joe was beside himself. He knew I was serious. Eventually, I compromised and told Joe I would strike a deal with him. I offered to do half the funeral and pastoral work if he would do the other half with me. I assured him that I would equip him to do his part. Once again, he reluctantly agreed.

You've never seen a more nervous man than Joe when he showed up at the funeral home for the service. But when all was said and done, though I perhaps was the more articulate speaker, without question Joe was the more effective minister. The reason is obvious— I didn't know this family. But Joe loved them and genuinely shared their pain.

Everyone needs such people in their lives. If a church grows as it should, one person could never be that close a friend to every member. And besides, even if he could, there would be no time to adequately equip the saints to do the work of ministry. If the pastor can (or thinks he can) do everything, why should the laity feel compelled to do anything?

THE COSTS

Having described the responsibilities that are part of the job description of the laymen in the church, we now look at the costs laypeople must be willing to pay in order to make all of this work. Jesus had some pointed things to say about the importance of counting costs before embarking on discipleship (Luke 14:25–33). In a similar sense, laity must pay the following costs:

1. *Allow the pastor and staff to be equippers.* It is not good enough to endorse the principle and then to hold oneself out as the exception to the rule. We must encourage our pastor and staff to be equippers. A congregation requires a great deal of patient training to reach this understanding. The old habits of direct pastoral care resist change. Wise laypeople will go out of their way to encourage equipping efforts undertaken by their pastor and staff.

2. *Readjust fellowship and leisure habits.* This relates to making time available. Some believers have their discretionary time so filled with fellowship activities, Bible study groups, hobbies, and sports that there is no time available to serve other people in their time of need. We certainly want others to be free to come to our aid during our times of crises. So, likewise, we have to make the time available to be ministers to our friends in need. Believers need to be trained by their leader's example and teaching to maintain a clear distinction between busyness and effectiveness.

3. *Follow God-ordained leadership with an attitude of trust.* The elders and staff give overall direction to the ministry in which laypeople are called to serve. Without an attitude of submission on the part of the laity, the service rendered will always be selective, dependent upon the degree of agreement with that overall direction. That does not mean that leadership can ride roughshod over their flock—laypeople's views are valuable and as often right as wrong. Laity should never be taught that they should remain quiet without strongly expressing their opinions about the direction of their church's ministry.

This third cost is difficult at times. Some who disagree with leaders choose the option to divorce God's church over disagreements about decisions made. (Please note that I don't believe that changing churches equates to divorcing the church. But changing churches over disagreements may be unwise and often indicates a lack of willingness to submit to God-given authority. By using the term *divorce* I am referring to terminating relationship with God's organized family over the decision of one church.)

Unfortunately, too many laypeople choose a second option in their relationship with the church. They resent decisions that don't go their way. They proudly express their determination to "stick it out," even as they carefully nurse their anger, hurt, and bitterness. It often becomes their mission to make life miserable for the leadership of God's church. God abhors such attitudes (Proverbs 6:16–19).

God has called His family to take a third option—a humble option. God exalts the humble and gives grace to those who practice healthy submission within the church. Life within a local body of Christ offers plenty of opportunities for the practice of mutual submission (Ephesians 5:21).

It is amazing to think of the potential unleashed in the family of God when each elder, deacon, pastor, staff member, and layperson not only discovers and implements the use of his or her spiritual gifts, but uses those gifts in the role to which God has called him or her. Clarifying such roles or job descriptions will ultimately be a blessing to God's people and an advantage in the advancement of His kingdom.

13

Inside the Effective Ministry Plan

7. STRATEGICALLY DESIGNED INFRASTRUCTURE

KEY QUESTION

—⚭—

HOW WILL WE STRUCTURE OUR CHURCH TO ACCOMPLISH OUR MISSION?

When I was a child, we sometimes played a game called Mr. Potato Head. Perhaps it's still being played today. In case you're not familiar with it, let me tell you how it works. You begin with a bare plastic "potato," which functions as a head. On one side of the potato you find two holes where the eyes should be and one hole each in the place of the mouth and nose. Included in the game box are several different sets of eyes and ears and several different noses and mouths. It's intriguing how different that potato-head face can look depending upon what combination is used.

For many years at our annual staff retreat we played a similar game with the infrastructure of our church. In fact, we called it "Mr. Potato Head." The holes in our plastic potato heads represented the prime times in the life of the church (Sunday morning being number one). The facial pieces represented the components of our infrastructure defined by our "what we do" values. By visualizing our suggested changes and priorities in this way, we were able not only to laugh at ourselves at times but also to discover some new looks for our ministry structure.

THE "PRIMARIES"

Outside the work of God's Spirit and the groundwork of consistent prayer, the three most significant factors influencing a ministry's success are *primary leadership, primary financial resources,* and *prime time*—that is, optimum times for scheduling of certain events. Time and thought spent plugging in the Potato Head parts of ministry—that is, structuring an organization so that the stated mission is accomplished—is time and thought well spent.

Additionally, leadership needs to answer certain key questions as they examine an existing infrastructure and propose changes. Will the church use Sunday morning as a time to worship, to reach non-believers, or to do both? Will the church be centralized or decentralized for most of its ministries? Will the church have a midweek centralized worship service or prayer meeting, or will it concentrate on decentralized groups throughout the week? And if the congregation is decentralized into small groups, will they be designed as discipleship groups or merely as care, share, and Bible study groups? When will leadership communities meet for training and equipping? What will be the structure to support adult education? When will it meet? Will Sunday night be used to gather again for worship, and if so, will it be an alternative service from that offered on Sunday morning or merely be a repeat service? Or will Sunday night be viewed as a time for all of God's people to slow down and enjoy their day of rest?

And then, what about specialized needs, such as youth and children? When will they meet and for what functions? Will the youth meet as a segregated ministry or will the ministry be structured as a pure cell church where youth, children, and adults stay together within the context of ministry?

When these questions, along with many related ones, have been dealt with adequately, you have defined your infrastructure.

PRIME TIME AND YOUR CHURCH

Every culture, and even community within a specific culture, defines its own prime time. The number one prime time for church activities in America differs from that in Japan. Suburbanites in North Atlanta define their number one prime time differently than the Bohemians in the same city do. It is important that the congregation's use of prime time lines up consistently with the church's previously determined "what we do" values.

This is exactly what seeker-service churches have done so well. They have set outreach as their highest "what we do" value and aligned it with their number one prime time, Sunday morning.

A caution is in order here. Be certain that any decision not to align worship with the Lord's Day is not a compromise of your biblical theology merely for the sake of practical functionality. It is not my intention to argue any position regarding the use of the Lord's Day or, for that matter, the priority of worship versus outreach. The rule must always be that God's Word is our infallible directive.

ABOUT LARGE CHURCHES

Can a Large Church Be Friendly?

Let's first consider the issue of size affecting friendliness. One of the widely held assumptions is that large churches are unfriendly. I'd like to challenge this notion, albeit with a smile. In fact, I have a suspicion that if this criticism is leveled accurately at any church, it should be leveled against the small church. This may, in part, account for why some churches remain small.

While vacationing one summer on the Florida coast, our family visited a small church in the community where we were staying. The church had a great reputation regarding its theological orthodoxy, but beyond this, I knew nothing about it. Because we didn't know what attire would be appropriate, we played conservative—the guys dressed in coat and tie and the girls put on dresses. Not certain about the worship service time, we arrived at 10:30 a.m. We misjudged on the side of caution in both ways—the dress was casual dress and the starting time was 11:00 a.m.

As we entered the building, we found that the foyer served as a fellowship hall. We had to walk through a roomful of people to enter the small sanctuary. They were having coffee and so-called "fellowship." It was obvious we were guests, if for no other reason than the six of us were the only people "dressed up" for the service. We immediately noticed that though people were looking over at us, no one approached to welcome us.

I decided to have some fun. I told Carol and the kids to stay by the door we had entered, and I took a stroll. I circled the room looking quickly from right to left, pretending to be looking for something. I was curious to see if I could provoke someone to be friendly or to ask if I needed help. If successful, I was going to ask for a bulletin. But my mission failed. When I arrived back at the starting point, I told Carol and the kids to follow me into the sanctuary. We walked through the middle of the crowd, took our seats, and waited twenty minutes or so as others took their seats. We left when the service was over, without ever being welcomed. So much for the claim that small churches are just naturally friendly!

> CELEBRATION IS ONE ACTIVITY OF THE LOCAL CHURCH THAT HAS POTENTIAL TO GET MORE DYNAMIC THE LARGER IT BECOMES.

Certainly, I know that many small churches are friendly and many large churches unfriendly. But the reverse is also true. In my opinion, we have nabbed the wrong villain. The culprit behind unfriendliness is not size but structure. Here's how it works:

Most churches begin as small churches. The small inner circle below can illustrate them. Within this small group flows excellent social engagement and community. Due to attractive programs, good preaching, or just simply the grace of God alone, the church begins to grow. The core, however, tends to remain a closed group. There's a certain practicality mixed with pride that assumes only members of the original group are qualified to be the keepers and guardians of the flame. Since most churches are structured in a centralized manner, people enter the outer life of the church through the large group gatherings. Most newcomers find it difficult, if not impossible, to break into the core group.

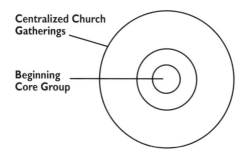

Let me describe a healthier structure. Assume the church to be a collection of small groups. These groups may be discipleship groups, prayer groups, service groups, neighborhood groups—whatever. Each week new groups are being started. These become important attraction and entry points for new people. Then, each week, the people from all these small groups gather collectively to worship. Worship is a celebration. The good news is that celebration is one activity of the local church that has potential to get more dynamic the larger it becomes.

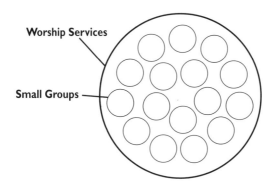

A Baseball Metaphor

Imagine being a fanatic Atlanta Braves fan in 1992. Just two years earlier your team was in last place. Now they are one game from being in the World Series. You've been waiting for this day as long as you can remember—the final game of the National League play-offs. You are sitting with your best friend and fellow maniac fan, George, in Atlanta-Fulton County Stadium. If Atlanta wins, it goes to the World Series.

It's the bottom of the ninth, Braves trailing Pittsburgh 2–1. With two outs and runners at second and third base, a hit means a victory for Atlanta. Francisco Cabrera is up to bat, and Sid Bream is on second, the go-ahead runner who has only one good leg. The outfield is playing in. The pitcher delivers. Cabrera swings. The sweet crack of the bat echoes and the ball sails over the shortstop's outstretched glove. The left fielder makes a clean pickup after one hop, even as the third-base coach is frantically waving Bream around third—teammate Dave Justice has already scored to tie the game. The throw whistles toward the catcher "on a rope." The ball and Bream will arrive at home plate at the exact same moment.

Bream slides. The tag sweeps across his body. It is a photo finish. Every eye is on the home plate umpire. An instant of silence settles on the stadium. And then, after what seems to be a little longer than forever, the umpire sweeps open his arms to declare Bream safe—and the Braves are on their way to the World Series.

The home crowd erupts in celebration. Cokes and beers spill; high fives, hugs, and jubilant shouts fill the air. People are kissing folks they have never met. As you and 53,000 other fans stand, you turn to George to celebrate with a high five. That's when you realize George is still sitting in his chair—emotionless.

You shout at him, "George, George, did you miss what happened? We won! We're going to the big one!" Yet George remains quiet and reserved, simply nodding in agreement. You ask, "What's the matter, George?"

Can you imagine him replying, "There are just too many people here to celebrate"? Of course not. In fact, usually, the bigger the crowd, the easier it is to lose oneself in celebration.

What we illustrated by the passing fortune of a sports team is infinitely more true of genuine worship. There are never too many people to celebrate the worth of God. My observation has been that, normally, as worship resources develop and expand in a church, there is also a heightened freedom to celebrate, making worship all the richer.

Certainly, I am not saying that the only reason for a centralized gathering of the church is for weekend worship services. But I am lobbying for the leadership of churches to consider what can be done best by the centralized church and what can be done better by the decentralized congregation. Such an evaluation will go a long way toward developing a healthy infrastructure.

Before I leave the issue of size, let me say a word about the size of small groups as it relates to function. A good rule of thumb is to remember that social needs are best defined by group *size*, whereas maturity needs are best defined by group *function*. In other words, if we want a newcomer in the church to be able to make much-needed social relationships, we put that person in a group large enough to have many options of new friends. Hopefully, that will allow him or her to find a few people who fit well as potential new friends. (And, by the way, the more evenly mixed male and female, the better.) But if we want to help someone grow deeply toward maturity in Christ, we want to put that person in a small group, no bigger than eight or ten. Such discipleship groups work best when they are gender specific—men with men and women with women.

FOUR "Cs"

Years ago, much was being made of church needing an infrastructure described by three words: cell, congregation, and celebration. These terms referred to a small group of five to seven, a midsized group of thirty to sixty, and then a group as large as you pleased for celebration.

My opinion is that such terms are misleading and miss the point. They suggest that if people find all three in their church (for example, a small group, a Sunday school class, and a worship gathering), their basic needs will be met. Not so. The terms speak of form but fail to address the bigger need, function.

I suggest we replace these three words with the following four terms (or similar ones) that address the real needs of our people.

1. *Celebration*—a daily personal and weekly corporate worship encounter with God
2. *Community*—supportive, accountable relationships with other believers
3. *Class*—a structured plan for understanding and applying the Word of God
4. *Commission*—an engagement with nonkingdom people with the intent of introducing them to Christ

When a Christian finds these functions taking place in her life, you can be certain that she is making advancement in her spiritual pilgrimage.

Since I have already tipped my hand regarding the value I place on discipleship, you might suspect that I would lobby strong for an infrastructure designed around a healthy worship experience and small groups that are discipleship oriented. Keep in mind that when I use the term *discipleship,* I am not using it in the broadest sense but in a more narrow use. I am referring to equipped leaders who labor in the life of few to the end of imparting not only the truth of God's Word but also the substance of their lives (1 Thessalonians 2:8). We will address this subject more specifically in chapter 20.

Now, having understood how to go about designing the church's infrastructure, we can move to the development of a culturally relevant strategy.

14

Inside the Effective Ministry Plan

8. CULTURALLY RELEVANT STRATEGY

KEY QUESTION

—〣—

HOW WILL WE ACCOMPLISH OUR MISSION?

Stories abound of companies that did not understand changes that were occurring in the culture and were eventually replaced by others who did. Consider the railroads. They were, at one time, among the most dominant of all companies in America. Unfortunately for them, they believed they were in the railroad business and not the transportation business and scoffed at the advent of air travel and did not understand the impact of the development of the interstate highway system.

Remember the name Smith Corona? It was one of the top brands in the typewriter business. Unfortunately for them, when the business community turned first to word processing systems and later to computer programs, they did not respond. With the strength of their brand name, had they kept pace with the ongoing advances in technology and moved into personal computers, Smith Corona might have become one of the larger word processing suppliers in the world.

Many in the film production business looked at the emergence of television and shrugged it off as a niche that would always be second to the theater. Of course, there are those who said, "Rock and roll is just a fad. It will never last." Both entertainment media have not only lasted, they have affected their "parents"—movies now feature television stars and versions of hit TV shows, while jazz and blues now incorporate elements of rock in their music.

Remaining culturally relevant is as critical to the church as it is for a large multinational company. A church's understanding of the culture is directly related to its ability to relate to the culture. It is at this phase of the planning process in which the ministry plan becomes individualized and targeted for a particular environment.

In case I haven't made it abundantly clear yet, my passion in ministry has a lot to do with discipleship. That priority remains unchanged no matter where I find myself. What has changed is the cultural factors that have influenced the way I practice discipleship. For example, I discovered the hard way that the almost unlimited opportunities to organize and practice discipleship I experienced in college were severely limited by the pressures and time constraints of life in the adult world. I had to rethink my methods of discipleship so that my passion would not become frustrated. For many of us, we don't have to look very far to realize that the world we are ministering in today is very different from the world many of us were born into.

THE CULTURE THEN AND NOW

Meet the 1950s

Allow me to make my point by contrasting the general culture of America in the 1950s with that of its culture at the turn of the millennium, fifty years later. At least three prominent descriptions can be made of American culture in the 1950s.

1. Our culture was accurately described as a Christian culture. This does not mean that a majority of people in America were Christians but that a majority of Americans held to Christian beliefs and/or values. For instance, if you conducted a random survey asking people's opinion about the appropriateness of allowing prayer in public schools, or of having the Ten Commandments in a federal building, virtually everyone asked would have responded that both should be allowed. If asked their opinion about a mother's right to end her pregnancy by means of abortion, the overwhelming majority would have said, "Absolutely not!" If asked whether they believed Jesus was the Son of God and the Bible the Word of God, again most people would have concurred.

2. *Our culture was slow paced.* Rarely did businessmen and businesswomen travel each week in their work. Commutes were shorter —and mainly made by men. The majority of women worked in their homes, and generally speaking, people stayed at home most every night. I can remember as a child being at home at night and suggesting to my parents that we go visit some friends who lived up the street. We didn't ever call to ask if it was convenient (after all, there was a good chance that the party line would be busy). We would jump in the car, drive to their home, and my brother or I would run to the door and receive the expected and welcomed invitation to come in to visit.

My wife, Carol, tells me that she rarely remembers a night when her entire family was not at home together (outside their being together at church or her father attending a monthly officers' meeting of his civic club). Without question, our culture was slow paced.

3. *Most families fit the "traditional" mold.* Some analysts have tagged households with "a working father, a homemaker wife/ mother, and two children under the age of eighteen as a 'traditional family.'" According to a survey of *Ministry Currents*, this four-person unit represented 60 percent of all American households in 1960.

Meet the 2000s

The culture today is almost diametrically opposed to the culture of the 1950s.

1. *Today's culture is best described as a secular culture.* Take the same "man on the street" interview and the responses would be dramatically opposite. Little needs to be said to substantiate this point. We've become much more secular. Christian values are often scorned or at best ignored.

2. *Today's culture is beyond fast paced.* Its pace could perhaps be described as supersonic! Carol and I love having people in our home. There's no telling how many guests come through our house annually. Even so, I recently asked her if she could remember a date in

recent history where it would be convenient for us to have someone "drop in" on us as my family did on others years ago. Every moment seems to be preassigned or committed to multiple activities.

3. Today's culture is no longer traditional-family oriented. Further statistics regarding the family indicate that about half of all marriages end in divorce. The divorce rate among subsequent marriages is even higher at 60 percent. It is reported that approximately two out of every five adults are divorced, separated, or widowed. And more than one-third of all senior citizens are widowed. Among those who will get married this year, more than six out of ten will live together before getting married. Cohabitation has literally mushroomed in the last few years.[1]

THE CULTURE THEN AND NOW

What about the church in light of these changes?

The Church of the 1950s

When I was a young student, I was introduced to the gospel at a church across the street from my childhood church. Because most people shared the same general Christian beliefs and values, most church attendees would state with confidence their affirmation of the Apostles' Creed. Everyone learned the Lord's Prayer in grade school and most could recite the Gloria Patri. So, most Protestant churches (the only church I am familiar with) had a similar order of worship, familiar to virtually all of its new attendees.

THE CULTURE OF AMERICA HAS CHANGED AND THE TYPICAL CHURCH HAS NOT.

Due to the slow pace of the culture, American churches had little outside competition for prime time. Because institutional social opportunities were at a minimum and because most people lived so close to their church, it was convenient to be at church twice on Sundays and at least once during the week (typically Wednesday night). With "Blue Laws" in effect—on Sundays nonessential businesses stayed closed and alcohol sales were banned—and a high view of the Lord's Day, neither the marketplace, nor sports leagues, nor recreational activities competed with the church or its people's time.

Fifty years ago, the church's menu had only about eight to ten offerings. In addition to Sunday morning worship and Sunday night services, the typical church had children's and adults' Sunday school, Wednesday night prayer meeting, choir, Boy Scouts and Girl Scouts, and women's circles. That was all that was necessary in light of the family support and stability found in the traditional family.

The Church of the New Millennium

Today the dynamic, growing church where I first heard the gospel is still faithful to the same message. Its orthodoxy has never changed—and neither has anything else! You can walk into this church today and feel you have stepped back in time—the same worship service, the same basic program offerings, and the same people, just older and grayer. This church today has approximately eighty people on an average Sunday, and the average age of those present is over eighty.

I'm sure this story could be echoed thousands of times over throughout the country. What has happened? The culture of America has changed and the typical church has not.

To illustrate what has happened, imagine with me that the most progressive and contemporary church you know was miraculously and entirely transplanted to Mongolia. Assume the people were supernaturally given the language of the Mongolian people, yet the music, programs, dress, and customs of the congregation remained unchanged. What would we expect to find fifty years later? We would probably find a tiny remnant group waiting to die off. We see the same condition in many churches in America today—churches that are out of touch with their culture and totally ineffective as a mission. Even their role as healthy, nurturing spiritual homes has been gradually replaced by a nostalgic repetition of old formulas that no longer affect the daily lives of the few who do attend.

Isn't it ironic that so many of these traditional churches, stuck in the past, would expect foreign missionaries to adapt to the culture of the people to whom they were sent to reach? They would insist upon these missionaries learning the language of these people, wearing the clothing, using the music and styles of their culture as well as the native instruments and architecture. The reality is that the culture of the America of the 1950s is almost as different from that of the new millennium as is the difference between the culture of

America and Mongolia. The problem is readily evident. The tradition-bound church does not really see itself as a mission—only as a home.

HOW CHURCHES GET STUCK

How do churches get stuck in time? Several lessons from human experience offer part of the explanation. The church has always struggled to do two things at the same time: maintain faithfulness to timeless truth (God's Word) while communicating the truth in a timely way and within a continually changing environment. Those challenges can get confused. A church that becomes too attached to a temporary style, as effective as it might at one time be, may end up actually devaluing the eternal truths it is charged to communicate. If the method becomes more important than the message or the audience, that church will not prevail.

Church leaders can profit considerably from studying the book of Acts while asking such questions as, "Why was it so difficult for Gentiles to enter the early church?" "In what ways did Peter, Paul, and others adapt their methods to the variety of situations in which they found themselves while maintaining a consistent gospel message?" "What parallel demands (healthy and unhealthy) do we place on people before we welcome them into the church?"

Methods that have worked in one setting can take on the mantle of universal applicability. A new lyric attached to a very familiar tune or music style may be used by God to transform a community. That effect, however, is not guaranteed if the lyric and tune are transplanted to a place where neither is familiar. Or, to put it another way, we find it very hard to imagine ourselves in a setting several hundred years ago in which "A Mighty Fortress Is Our God" or Handel's *Messiah* were cutting-edge, contemporary music looked at suspiciously by many.

We can't place ourselves four hundred years in the past to listen to a heated discussion about a dangerous and possibly heretical new translation of the Bible into a crude and debased language like English, only to realize the subject under discussion is the King James Version. We must remember the methods and means that may seem to us unchangeable were once the latest thing.

An initial environment of change is attractive to most people. People who are outsiders don't mind change as long as it results in their inclusion. Yet once they become insiders, people tend to resist change, wanting to keep things the way they were when they were attracted. Therefore, the church's leadership often hears its constituency in essence say, "If you change, I will leave." Unfortunately, few people are speaking up for the lost community who are thinking, at least subconsciously, "If you don't change, I won't come."

People tend to think things will stay the same if nothing is changed. They underestimate the pervasive presence of change in the world. Keeping things externally "the same" hardly prevents change. The changes simply occur in more subtle and devastating ways. So a church may keep doing what it has always done before, but the effectiveness and meaning of those practices will probably be radically altered. If we want to maintain the same allegiance to the truth, the same effectiveness in communication, and the same faithfulness to our purpose, we must continually change.

G. K. Chesterton once illustrated this point by talking about what happens when you build a white picket fence in your yard. If you want to keep that picket fence the same as when you built it, the worst thing you can do is leave it alone. You must change it constantly— checking, repairing, and repainting it.[2] Faithful church boards understand that if they don't give constant attention to the church facilities, the buildings will eventually fall down. Why are we so reluctant to apply the same principle to the body of Christ that meets in those facilities?

Being contemporary simply means studying one's culture accurately and then asking what can be done, without compromising any convictions or biblical standards, to eliminate barriers to reaching the unchurched community

UNDERSTANDING YOUR COMMUNITY AND CULTURE

The first step in developing culturally relevant strategies for your community is to take the time to learn about the community you serve. There are a number of factors that you should investigate.

What is their faith background? Are they largely unchurched or people who attended church when they were younger but fell away? What was their church affiliation? How you speak to people who were raised Roman Catholic and who fell away from the church would be somewhat different from how you speak to people who had been part of a mainline denominational church.

For those who do not currently attend church, what is it that keeps them from attending? The seeker-sensitive church movement began over thirty years ago as churches began to ask questions to determine why people didn't attend church. Three primary barriers were identified: (1) church was boring and it was largely irrelevant to their day-to-day lives; (2) the music was dull and uninspiring; and (3) churches were always asking for money. In response, this new generation of churches began reconnecting with their communities through contemporary music and thematic drama, biblical teaching with an emphasis on life application, and making a point of telling its visitors that giving was only for people who called this church home.

What questions or issues do they deal with as it relates to coming to faith in Jesus Christ? Do they believe that all faiths lead to heaven? Do they believe that God exists? Do they resist God because they don't understand how a loving God allows the hurt and pain in the world today?

What are the needs of the people in the community that you serve? For example, is there an above-average number of blended family couples who need and would benefit from marriage and parenting support? Do you live in a community that has a high level of turnover and whose people would benefit from a ministry that helped them get to know and get connected in the community? Do you have a higher-than-average population of single-parent families? Do you have a higher than average number of families with young children?

Visit churches in your area that are growing. Are they reaching the same demographic group that you are reaching? What styles of worship do they offer? What type of outreach ministries do they have?

While the focus of information outlined above discussed identifying the needs of people within the community, you should also take time to learn about your own congregation. Complete a demographic profile of your congregation, including information about the neighborhoods and areas they live in and the schools their children attend. You should learn about their spiritual background, what drew them to your church, and their views about the strengths and weaknesses of the church. You should work to determine what needs they have that are not currently being met by the church.

If you are a church that gets the names of visitors and you have the ability to know the names of people who have visited but chose not to make your church their home, you could make a follow-up phone call or visit to the people to get feedback. In making these types of calls or visits, it is important to communicate to the people that the purpose of your call is to learn about their experience with your church so that you can learn and improve, and not about trying to "twist their arm" into coming back.

Research and asking questions are valuable tools for learning about your community. Information can be gathered about the community through tools available on the Internet or something as simple as just observing the changes that are taking place in your community. Valuable information can be gathered from people in your church about the changes that are taking place in the community. We have tapped into businesspeople in our church who are engaged in real estate development within our region. They know much about the shifts that are taking place.

You can also utilize Internet blogs to engage in conversations with people who may be outside of the church. We host an event we call Investigative Forum several times a year where we open the doors of the church to our community to have an open microphone discussion with me. I get a strong sense of where the hearts of the people of our community are in those sessions. Finally, for me personally, personal evangelism offers insight into what seems to be on the minds and hearts of the people in our community. Nothing can replace that one-on-one interaction with an unchurched person to gain the freshest insight into the secular mind.

Keeping your finger on the pulse of your community and culture is not a onetime event. It is something that needs to be done on a continuing basis. I honestly think that the best way to know and understand the community is to have your members interacting with the unchurched where they live, work, and play. Ultimately, engaging the unchurched on their ground is fieldwork that surpasses any textbook research you might seek to do. If we are among the unchurched, building relationships, this will give rise to the opportunity for God to do His work of transformation. I have observed that God often uses His Word and exposure to His people to bring about change in the lives of men and women.

Before we move to the ninth component of an effective ministry plan, I challenge you to give serious thought to four questions that will finalize your culturally relevant strategy. The next chapter goes inside culturally relevant strategies to consider four key questions. Failure to carefully consider these questions will leave a gap in your thought process and could leave a significant gap in your ministry plan.

Notes

1. These statistics have been widely reported. Their implications have been explored in such works as *Complete Marriage and Family Home Reference Guide,* by James Dobson (Wheaton: Tyndale, 2000); *Loving Solutions,* by Gary Chapman (Chicago: Northfield, 1988); and many others. See also "Christians Are More Likely to Experience Divorce than Are Non-Christians," Barna Research Group, 21 December 1999; and "Born Again Adults Less Likely to Co-Habit, Just as Likely to Divorce," Barna Research Group, 6 August 2001; both articles accessed at barna.org Web site.

2. As quoted in Joe Garlington, "Finding the Grace Gates," *Leadership Journal* (spring 1999).

15

Inside Culturally Relevant Strategies

FOUR QUESTIONS THAT MUST NOT BE OVERLOOKED

In the previous chapter, we discussed the importance of understanding your community and developing strategies and plans that are relevant to the culture that God has called you to serve. In this chapter, we turn our attention to four universal questions that must be addressed in the development of a ministry plan regardless of the size or location of your church. They are:

1. In what ways and to what degree will the unchurched be reached and hurting people helped?
2. In what ways and to what degree will new people be folded into the family of God?
3. In what ways and to what degree will God's people learn biblical truth?
4. In what ways and to what degree will people be shepherded?

Let's consider each question in turn.

QUESTION ONE: HOW DO WE REACH THE UNCHURCHED AND HELP THE HURTING?

There's a familiar saying, "There are many ways to skin the cat!" Well, the same applies to reaching the unchurched. Any one, or better yet, many or all of the following approaches are options that can be used. The choice becomes, which one or ones will the church embrace? And if multiple approaches are the answer, which one gets the greater investment of resources? Five of the most effective options include: worship, outreach events, small groups, specialty programs, and community bridge building.

Worship Services

Today churches face a dizzying array of options for structuring their worship services. Will they be seeker friendly? Will they be traditional? Will they be contemporary? Will they target the postmodern or Gen-X? Will they seek to entertain members? The options go on and on.

Often, I will have a potential church planter call me to talk about starting a new church. I typically ask him to describe the church he plans to plant. After I listen to his description, regardless of the characteristics, I respond positively—yet with a well-worn follow-up question: "What are the downsides to such a strategy?" Unfortunately, the usual response is a blank stare and the admission that he has not considered any downsides. The point, of course, is that every strategy has its downside. By choosing one specific road, you have also chosen many roads you will not travel. Every action you decide to take involves a number of actions you have decided not to take.

In a later chapter, I will specifically address the issue of hard decisions on continuum issues. But let me summarize what will be explained later: Continuum choices (modern and postmodern; traditional and contemporary; seeker and believer) usually create contrasting weaknesses. Typically, the following questions need to be addressed regardless of the model that a pastor suggests he is considering:

- For whom is worship designed?
- Will you deploy a small-group strategy?
- How will you raise and train leaders?
- When will Christians get educated?
- Will there be alternatives for believers who are unable to make the stated worship time?
- How many times per week can a typical family be involved in church activities and still be functionally stable?

The pie of time is only so big. You can cut it many different ways, but every slice devoted to one value takes away time from another important value. The adage often rings true, "If it's too good to be true, it's too good to be true." No strategy choice is without downsides. The culture, particular demographics of people being reached, and the gift mix of church leadership are both important factors in deciding which strategy to use.

Those church planters who claim to hold to the high values of worship and equipping the saints must be relatively certain that their strategy actually allows those values to be experienced in the church. The strategy must also be effective in a way that fits today's modern culture while also speaking to the unchurched. Never allow pragmatic zeal (even for such a lofty value as reaching the lost) to be motivation for theological compromise regardless of the strategy you choose.

Sound biblical worship can reach the nonbeliever simply by being sensitive to the nonbeliever's presence, carefully choosing language that the unchurched can relate to, and by creatively applying the preaching of God's Word to the lost as well as to believers. Corporate worship is designed for the believer, but when done in an authentic way can be stimulating to the lost, causing them to want to continue attending. It is then that God often uses the constant exposure to His Word and His people to bring His chosen into His fold. The biggest challenge for a pastor and his leadership team is to understand God's vision for their church, not what the latest success-oriented program is that is making the rounds in the church community.

Outreach Events

These are churchwide events in which it is easy for members of your church to invite people to attend. Many churches develop and host events at Christmas and Easter, two times during the year when unchurched people are most likely to attend church.

As I mentioned in the last chapter, each year we hold Investigative Forums, where our unchurched friends and people in the community can come and ask their questions. We have been surprised at the candor and sincerity of those asking questions. By respecting those who bring the questions (creating a friendly, nonthreatening environment) and seeking to offer honest answers, we have seen many who have become followers of Christ and/or regular attendees to our worship services. You can find out more about the investigative forum on our Web site.

Small Groups

There is no better environment for equipping and accountability than a small group. Thus, such groups become excellent vehicles to win the lost. Groups could be evangelistic (inviting the unchurched to attend), or they could be equipping stations to launch individual believers into the mission fields in which they live, work, and play.

Specialty Programs

Addressing the crisis needs of people in common struggles has proven to be an effective way of reaching nonbelievers. Programs for those dealing with alcohol and drug addiction, AIDS, cancer, crisis pregnancy, the death of a loved one, or divorce—all are designed to help people through difficult times and are great opportunities to introduce them to Christ.

One nationally recognized program designed by one of our former staff members, Bob Burns, called "Fresh Start," has been a tremendous tool for reaching the lost. People who have experienced the pain of separation and divorce are invited to a weekend seminar. Following the seminar, they are invited to continue meeting weekly with a support group of people in common crisis known as "Genesis." The program is nothing more than the application of the saying, "Find a need and fill it." But as the need is being addressed, the One who alone can and will meet their deepest needs is introduced. Such specialty programs are valuable tools for reaching the lost.

Individual Equipping

Suffice it to say that believers need to experience two significant areas of training to become effective ministers to others:

1. They must see their pastors and leaders practicing the disciplines of the spiritual life, particularly the sharing of their faith with others on a personal basis. This is training by modeling.
2. They must be equipped, encouraged, and expected to share their faith with others as one of the primary expressions of their growth in discipleship.

These two areas must be addressed in conscious ways if a church is serious about prevailing.

Community Bridge Building

Meeting needs where people live is certainly part of "Specialty Programs" mentioned above, but it's also part of community bridge building. About two years prior to celebrating our twenty-fifth anniversary as a church, we sought to understand what adjustments in our ministry needed to be made as we launched into our second quarter of a century.

Our elders urged me to come with whatever recommendations for change I thought necessary, regardless of how radical they might be. As I shared my ideas, most of which related to "giving ourselves away for the sake of the least and the lost," one of our staff members handed me a book, saying, "You've got to read this book. It's just what you are talking about." That was my introduction to *The Church of Irresistible Influence*, by Robert Lewis, a book I have commended earlier.

Robert says with clarity and experience what every church, including ours, needs to learn. This book, plus Tim Keller's book *Ministries of Mercy* (R&R Publishing), helped to shape our church's future strategy to build bridges from our church into the communities in which we live, work, and play—all with the intention of allowing our deeds to speak to people's needs as loudly as our words.

So the first question that must be answered in forming a culturally oriented strategy is, "In what ways and to what degree will the unchurched be reached and hurting people be helped?" Regardless of the strategy chosen, just make sure that reaching the unchurched remains a priority.

QUESTION TWO: HOW DO WE ASSIMILATE NEW PEOPLE INTO THE FAMILY OF GOD?

We can look at many ways to bring people into God's family, yet perhaps more important than the *choice* of strategy is the very *existence* of a strategy that everyone can understand and have confidence in. An assimilation strategy shouldn't necessarily be equated with merely getting people into membership. Assimilation can be achieved both by getting attendees relationally connected to others in the church and by giving attendees ownership of the ministry where they feel they can make a valuable contribution. Both these endeavors can be challenging tasks.

In part because of the fast-paced society in which we live today, deep relationships are hard to come by—and according to many people, it's up to the churches to provide those relationships. Not so! It is the believer's own responsibility to build personal relationships. It is not uncommon today for an insecure spouse to feel unloved by a very loving and adoring mate. Yet past relational experiences have conditioned them to believe they are unlovable. Thus, regardless of the love demonstrated, it cannot be received. Likewise, among those entering churches, opportunities for meeting people do not automatically guarantee deep relationships. In addition to the problems created by individual insecurities, the fast pace of modern life makes relationship building difficult. Chuck Swindoll famously said, "Busyness rapes relationships" *(Killing Giants, Pulling Thorns)*. And it is so true. Regardless of how you cut it, a large investment of time is required to produce meaningful relationships.

All this to say: Church leaders should not beat themselves up when newcomers find it hard to make relationships. Yet it is wise to develop a strategy that makes it as easy as possible to get relationally connected.

Groups of different sizes provide a variety of relational options. As mentioned in the previous chapter, the larger the group, the more opportunity the group provides socially because there are more options for people to meet and connect. The smaller the group, the deeper the relationship can go due to vulnerable sharing and caring for one another. But any way you look at it, small- to medium-sized groups (five to fifty) are great forums to help establish relationships.

Another rule of thumb to follow is that new people assimilate best with new people. After a while, people in a group fill their relational cups (especially those in a season of life with multiple young children). Group members may have good intentions about reaching out to newcomers, yet long-term groups tend to display what might be called "institutional neglect." Smiles and handshakes may be abundant, but little to no room is left over for new relationships. So, try as hard as they may, it is typically difficult for people to break in to longtime existing groups. A wise strategy is to continually form new groups.

In addition to offering a variety of sizes of groups, it also helps in assimilation to offer a variety in the types of groups. We have found that if we provide three types of small groups, everyone can find a group that fits with his or her needs and/or wants. We offer fellowship, service, and equipping groups. Each type of group majors in that which its name implies and minors in the other two functions. For instance, a service group majors in serving and minors in fellowship and growth.

Our fellowship groups vary in size and activities. They are not high-commitment groups, but offer informal entry points to congregational life. They function much as Sunday school classes function in many churches. Their names give some clue to their identity: Neighborhood Congregations, Seasons of Life Communities, and Home Fellowships. These groups are not designed as ends but as beginning places for participation in the whole life of the church.

HAVING A SENSE OF CONTRIBUTING TO THE MISSION OF THE CHURCH IS A GOOD WAY TO GET ASSIMILATED.

Our service groups are divided into three types: (1) those that serve during the weekend services; (2) those that provide ministries within our church; and (3) those that serve people who have needs within the communities in which we live, work, and play. Each group has a shepherd to offer care to all the group members.

Among our equipping groups, the most important are what we call Discipleship Teams. Each Discipleship Team has a leader who goes through training on Sunday mornings and is under the leadership and care of a coach. Each coach is under the leadership and care of a staff pastor.

All three types of groups are important. God calls us to different places in various seasons of our lives. Such a variety of offerings assures an opportunity for each individual to find his or her best fit.

As I have already mentioned, having a sense of contributing to the mission of the church is a good way to get assimilated. Making it easy to find a task (especially one that employs one's spiritual gifts, talents, and interests) lessens the difficulty of getting assimilated. Working side by side with fellow believers in ministry is an excellent way to make lasting friendships.

To help our people get assimilated, we introduce them to what we call "connecting points." These points highlight the primary means by which most of our people will establish relationships and find an opportunity to make a contribution to the mission of the church.

The connecting points include six important components:

1. Attending weekend worship services
2. Joining the church
3. Serving in a ministry
4. Joining a small group
5. Taking Perimeter's membership equipping courses (to be explained later)
6. Taking Perimeter's leadership training courses (and assuming ministry leadership along with ongoing training)

This list captures the intentionality and the progression in our strategies. The intentional church has specific strategies for assimilating new people into God's family.

QUESTION THREE: HOW DO GOD'S PEOPLE LEARN BIBLICAL TRUTH?

Several years ago, we invited Roberta Hestenes, then president of Eastern College, to do a seminar at our church on small groups. One of the comments she made that I'll never forget was that she feared the impact of the modern church-growth movement on the church of future generations. Her question: "With the popular models for church today, when and where will people learn the Bible? Where will people learn the book of Isaiah?" What a challenge!

There are numerous ways to answer these concerns. The four I've included represent what we consider our most strategic responses to this pressing need.

The Pulpit

Many pastors, especially those coming out of a Reformed tradition in theology, bank almost solely on the pulpit for educating their people. The strength of this tradition is the high view of the Scriptures and the dependence upon the work of the Holy Spirit. Yet as we have seen earlier, Scripture places much emphasis on the additional value of truth being conveyed in a relational context (what I call life-on-life).

Even while we embrace a high view of preaching, we must also admit that the preaching of God's Word can be either effective or ineffective. Both what is said and how it is said play significant roles in determining effectiveness.

After affirming that the truth of God's Word is to be the substance of one's preaching, the next priority is to determine one's goal for preaching. Is the goal primarily to educate God's people? Or is the goal to challenge God's people? Or is it both, or even something else? Is it directed to seekers, young believers, or mature believers?

I am convinced that the goal of preaching should be to bring God's Word to bear upon people in every stage of spiritual pilgrimage in such a way as to bring every person under the lordship of Christ in every area of life.

I believe that for approximately the first ten years of my ministry I had an improper understanding of the purpose of my preaching. My shift in understanding is perhaps best captured in one of my journal notes in July of 1990:

> *To aim at a Bible passage as one preaches, periodically making applications to personal life, will leave the believing community convinced they have been taught by God's man. But to aim at a personal life while preaching, bringing God's truth to bear upon its need, will leave the believing community convinced they have been taught by God's Spirit.*

My understanding of preaching was much impacted by the teaching of Haddon Robinson, who wrote:

Life-changing preaching does not talk to people about the Bible. Instead, it talks to people about themselves (their questions, lusts, fears and struggles) from the Bible. The basic principle in preaching is to give as much biblical information as the people need to understand the passage, and no more. Then move on to your application. When we approach the sermon with that philosophy, flint strikes steel. The flint of someone's problems strikes the steel of the Word of God, and a spark ignites that can set that person on fire for God.[1]

I am discouraged to see how often intellectual stimulation is more desired than spiritual vitalization. Though preaching must certainly be intellectually challenging, it can never be the goal in sight.

Especially since the early 1970s, there has been much debate concerning the appropriate approach to preaching. When I began pastoral ministry, those I admired the most championed expositional teaching through books of the Bible as the "most biblical approach." Topical preaching was viewed as significantly inferior, if even acceptable at all. The lack of compelling reasons for such a conclusion, in addition to examples of great preachers of the past, such as Charles Spurgeon, who didn't always preach through books of the Bible, left me with skepticism.

When I attended seminary, in addition to approximately one-third of our time spent studying practical theology, about one-third of the curriculum was given to biblical theology (learning the text verse by verse). The other one-third of our curriculum concentrated on systematic theology (studying the topics of God's Word by drawing upon texts throughout the Bible). It appeared to me then, as it does to me these years later, that expository preaching is nothing more than preaching that concentrates on biblical theology, whereas topical preaching focuses on systematic theology. It seems to me that each is equally valuable to sound preaching. They reinforce each other.

There is a third category of preaching that is a blend of the two—perhaps we could call it topical exposition. An illustration of this would be preaching on a topic such as celibacy but doing so simply by expositing what Paul had to say to the people of Corinth in his first epistle.

Perhaps some preachers would decide that they can best steward their teaching or exhortation gifts by primarily doing one of the preaching approaches. I personally enjoy them all, finding my typical year's preaching calendar divided, giving approximately 25 percent to expository preaching, 25 percent to topical teaching, and 50 percent to topical exposition.

I would suggest that every church make sure that there is balance in the full offerings of the church. If the pastor primarily teaches using expository preaching, make sure that topical study of the Word is offered elsewhere in the life of the church.

Church members often get disgruntled at the approach their pastor uses when he preaches. They remember well how they grew so quickly as a new Christian under a particular approach and now assume that their lack of continued spiritual growth is due to their pastor's using a different approach.

Let me illustrate the absurdity of such a conclusion. I am of average height, and so are my wife and both of our families. It appeared throughout his childhood as though Matt, our first child, would be the same. However, when he was fifteen, he experienced an unusual growth spurt and ended up being six foot three inches (extremely tall for a Pope). During the next couple of years, people constantly asked him, "How'd you get so tall, boy?" If he answered accurately, his response would have been, "Eating pizza." That seemed to be all he wanted at that age (and I'm sure we gave in far too often). Matt could have easily concluded that if everyone else ate primarily pizza at age fifteen they too would grow tall.

Well, we know better. The truth is that we are all genetically wired to grow to a certain height. Only malnutrition will significantly alter our genetic wiring. The reality is that regardless of what Matt ate, as long as he was getting an adequate intake of nutrients, he was destined to grow to his genetically coded height.

So, too, with the Word of God. The Word causes us to grow regardless of how it is served. Most hearers have their preferred styles, but this does not invalidate other styles.

Having argued for the importance of preaching, I would suggest that preaching is not enough in and of itself to provide sufficient education for God's people. Let's look at some other forums for teaching the full counsel of God.

The Classroom

There are many different uses of the classroom in training believers, but perhaps the most familiar is Sunday school. Every exposure to God's Word is valuable, but most would agree that adult Sunday school is less than ideal for education. Many people are primarily motivated to attend for relational reasons. Few are willing to do outside study in preparation for their class. Add to this that a typical class has a widely varying attendance from week to week and a diverse audience spiritually (eager infant Christians, long-term believers with little appetite for growth, and extremely mature followers). Given these conditions, quality education is difficult at best. These reasons also explain why so many people who have attended adult Sunday schools for a lifetime are nevertheless biblically illiterate.

Elective courses designed with homework assignments are often better vehicles to help people gain biblical information. Whether in week-to-week or concentrated seminar fashion, the classroom can play a valuable role in the Christian's biblical education.

Small Groups

If one evaluates education based on what is learned rather than by what is taught, small groups will be viewed as an ideal forum for education. Perhaps this would be accepted as the norm if we had an abundance of able and willing instructors. Few, if any, churches have enough knowledgeable, gifted communicators to supply large numbers of small groups with teachers. But modern technology has alleviated some of the constraints created when education depends on the teacher alone to deliver the truth. By using study books, tapes, and well-written curriculum, good education can take place in small groups of any size church.

Whether studying books of the Bible or topics related to Christian living or theology, small groups can be excellent vehicles for Christian education.

Personal Study

In my opinion, by far the best way to learn biblical truth is through personal study. Such learning can take place through daily personal worship as well as through regular personal Bible study. I have often said that I have learned more at the Bedside School of the Bible than I ever learned in all the seminars, Sunday school classes, Bible conferences, and seminary classes I attended combined.

Much like learning to do evangelism well, believers need to learn one primary approach or method for partaking of Christ's truth that best serves them. Such personal worship and study methods need to be included in the equipping provided in the church's discipleship ministry.

These are just four of many different venues for learning biblical truth. Developing a culturally relevant strategy will require you to determine to what extent you will use these or other means.

QUESTION FOUR: HOW DO WE SHEPHERD GOD'S PEOPLE?

In what ways and to what degree will we shepherd God's people? Ask pastors what their approach to shepherding is and you will often hear them describe a new approach they are initiating to replace a plan that has not worked well. Candidly, shepherding the flock is more like keeping up with cats than sheep. They often move quickly, can be very evasive, and are sometimes so temperamental they don't want to be petted.

But God leaves no room for dismissal of this task. Peter, speaking under inspiration of God, says to elders, "Shepherd the flock of God among you, exercising oversight not under compulsion, but voluntarily, according to the will of God; and not for sordid gain, but with eagerness; nor yet as lording it over those allotted to your charge, but proving to be examples to the flock" (1 Peter 5:2–3).

In the book of Hebrews, God speaks soberly to us when the author, addressing believers, says, "Obey your leaders and submit to them, for they keep watch over your souls as those who will give an account" (Hebrews 13:17).

A Reasonable Plan

So how does a church do a good job of keeping up with its people so as to care for them well? Like most endeavors that are successful, there needs to be a plan to accomplish the task. Such workable plans can be constructed around geography, seasons of life, small groups, and other grouping categories. The important thing is that the span of care is reasonable in size; the leadership responsible for shepherding is qualified, well trained, and faithful to the task; and those in shepherding positions are cared for themselves. It is certainly ideal to align one's shepherding strategy as closely as possible to discipleship (as discipleship is indeed the purest form of shepherding). But realistically, many within the church family will not be in discipleship groups.

Because each church and culture (racial, economic, and geographical) is so different, I will not suggest one grouping category to be superior over the others. However, I do believe that every individual in the church who desires to be shepherded should have a specifically designated leader responsible for that task. Members should be responsible to participate in the worship and work of the church. Their unwillingness to do so should rightly cause them to forfeit the more mature levels of care and shepherding that people need. Those responsibilities and privileges should be carefully spelled out for those in membership. (Our church uses the membership questions written by the Westminster Divines in the 1600s that include a promise "to participate in the worship and work of the church.")

We now structure our ministry in such a way that all people could be in some form of small group unless providentially hindered by health or unique circumstances (and then special care must be offered). Whether in a fellowship, service, or equipping group, someone is designated as a leader of the group and carries the responsibility of being a shepherd to those who participate. This means that every volunteer in our church should be cared for by a leader.

It is of utmost importance that each leader is cared for by a shepherd (some call those coaching shepherds), and if the organization is large enough, those coaching shepherds must be shepherded by a pastor (usually a staff member or a lay pastor).

Shepherding goals are critical measuring rods to determine how noncrisis care is being accomplished. Those goals could include the following:

- Implementing the church's "who we are" values (for example, love, integrity, faith, and truth)
- Evaluating those being discipled by using the description of a mature and equipped follower of Christ (for example, "Live under the direction of the Word of God, the control of the Holy Spirit, and the compelling love of Christ")
- Meeting the participation goals set by the church (for example, consistent worship, church membership, and small-group participation)

Corrective Shepherding

Corrective shepherding is ultimately only as good as the willingness of the church leadership to discipline erring members. God has given the "keys to the kingdom to elders" to be used when needed. Those keys must sometimes be used to unlock membership doors, so as to allow unrepentant members to be dismissed from membership ("Treat him as you would a pagan," Matthew 18:17 NIV). I am grieved to see how few churches, otherwise known to be great churches, are unwilling to exercise this means of grace to those who are in need of it.

Though biblical shepherding may be difficult, it is absolutely imperative—from noncrisis loving care and concern, to crisis care, to restorative church discipline. Would that the church once again claim its full responsibilities in this endeavor.

Note

1. As quoted in Scott Gibson, *Making a Difference in Preaching* (Grand Rapids: Baker, 1990), 94.

16

Inside the Effective Ministry Plan

9. WELL-DEVELOPED GOALS AND PLANS

KEY QUESTION

—⚻—

HOW WILL WE KNOW WE ARE ACCOMPLISHING OUR VISION AND MISSION?

You have probably heard the expression, "How do you eat an elephant?" and its corresponding answer, "One bite at a time." In developing an effective ministry plan, we have has been breaking a faith-oriented, God-sized, "unless God be in it" vision statement into smaller and smaller pieces in order to create a set of plans that break the vision into manageable, bite-size pieces. Here's how we do that:

- Break down the vision statement into big-picture component parts of a mssion statement that answers the question: "How will we achieve our vision?"
- Break down those components of the mission statements into SMART goals that answer the question: "How will we accomplish our mission?" SMART is an acronym for goals that are *specific, measurable, attainable, realistic,* and *time bound;* they will be discussed in the section "Smart Goals."

- Finally, break down each SMART goal into specific action plans, timelines, responsibilities, resources, and budgets.

ARE GOALS UNBIBLICAL?

Many faithful followers of Christ have argued that goals are inappropriate tools. "Goals," they have said, "presume upon God and seek to make man's ways, God's ways. Goals attempt to control and perhaps quench the Holy Spirit. Goals limit God."

To the contrary, it would be fairer to say that a *lack* of goals actually limits God's work more than goal setting. Even the simplest goals get a life or a group in motion. Lack of goals leaves a life's and a group's transmission set in "Park." Even if the goals are not accurate, they serve in such a way to validate the saying, "It's easier to steer a vehicle in motion than it is to steer a parked car."

The concept of goals is certainly not foreign to the Scriptures. Jesus Himself, in response to warnings of danger from Herod, said, "Go and tell that fox, 'Behold, I cast out demons and perform cures today and tomorrow, and the third day I reach My goal'" (Luke 13:32). The apostle Paul refers to man's ultimate goal in Philippians 3:14, "I press on toward the goal for the prize of the upward call of God in Christ Jesus."

Paul's blend of moving toward a goal yet being submissive to whatever the Lord might have in store for him appears at the close of 1 Corinthians. Paul wrote, "I will come to you after I go through Macedonia, for I am going through Macedonia. . . . For I do not wish to see you now just in passing; for I hope to remain with you for some time, *if the Lord permits*. But I will remain in Ephesus until Pentecost" (1 Corinthians 16:5, 7–8, emphasis added).

In speaking to the crowds of people who were following Him, Christ challenged them to count the cost of following, just as a builder evaluates his plans to determine the cost before beginning construction so that he would not begin a project that he could not afford to complete (see Luke 14:25–33). He also cited the example of a king assessing his opportunity to win before going into a battle against another king. If, after assessing the situation he determined that he cannot win, the king will ask for terms of peace while the other king's army is still a long way off.

Even a well-known passage such as James 4:13–15, which is sometimes quoted to discourage goal setting, actually encourages it. The passage starts out with what appears to be a devastating attack on goal setting: "Now listen, you who say, 'Today or tomorrow we will go to this or that city, spend a year there, carry on business and make money.' Why, you do not even know what will happen tomorrow. What is your life? You are a mist that appears for a little while and then vanishes" (NIV).

But in the end, even while reproving any tendency to disregard God's will in goal setting—"You ought to say, 'If it is the Lord's will'"—it acknowledges the need for plans and goals: "We will live *and do this or that*" (v. 15, emphasis added).

Goal setting enables us to put expression and direction to an act of faith. Goals are simply targets. They are not to be viewed as dictates from God. They can be changed and even missed without shame. We never forget that our goals set us in motion, but we fully expect God to steer the vehicle.

"WHAT ARE THE NEXT STEPS GOD WANTS US TO TAKE IN THE PROCESS?"

Goals help set the stage for action. As the authors of the book *Built to Last* have written, they are critical for "stimulating progress . . . [and] protecting a company's core ideology and the type of progress it aims to achieve."[1] They enable us to have a better sense of direction and purpose while allowing us to evaluate our progress. They help us to plan ahead and communicate within the organization. Without goals, those involved in the mission don't have a clear understanding of what is expected.

SMART GOALS

Goals will ultimately be decided by answering the question, "How will we know if we are making progress toward accomplishing our vision and mission?" Goals represent the mile markers and signposts that tell us how we are doing. Using the familiar acronym SMART to describe goals is a good way to make sure that the goals being set are helpful. They must be Specific, Measurable, Attainable, Realistic, and Time Bound.

Specific

In chapter 2 we looked at seven factors that always have an impact on the growth of a local church. The fifth factor we listed as adequate property, facilities, and parking. Let's use these for examples of goal setting. Once you have decided what those requirements will mean in your setting, you will need to set down the incremental steps that will take you from your present situation to a plan the leadership will agree is adequate for accomplishing your vision and mission. "A big building and lots of parking" is not a good example of specific goals.

You need to decide what your requirements are, and how you will get from here to there: space for a specific number of cars, an educational wing that includes kitchen facilities and a large fellowship room to accommodate a specific number of people, and more. Aim at being specific and you will tend to hit clarity.

Measurable

Motives, assumptions, and expectations all become clearer as we discuss the measurability of our goals. For instance, the goal at Unite! is to partner with one hundred congregations in the northeast Atlanta area in the next three years and to identify one anchor church in the northwest quadrant in the next twelve months. It is important that the vision be broken down into yearly increments, with appropriate adjustments being made along the way.

Attainable

Healthy goal setting includes a conscious effort to express a vision in doable steps. The vision, by definition, has the appearance of implausibility and the characteristic, hopefully, of being so big that it is "doomed to failure unless God be in it." Without ever forgetting for a moment that God ultimately makes it happen, we must still answer the question, "What are the next steps God wants us to take in the process?" A goal needs to include specific actions we can actually take.

Realistic

Realists often come across as pessimists. Most elder boards include at least one realist. A board made up exclusively of either idealists or realists is a frightening creature, but a healthy mix makes for good goal setting. Realists in church leadership keep the steps from being too big. Many goals could be described as attainable even though may not be realistic. One hundred percent of the congregation's members tithing may be attainable as a goal in the sense that they all *could* tithe, but not realistic if the present reality is 10 percent of the members of the church tithe. But increasing the current number of tithers to 20 percent would make a measurable impact on many aspects of church life.

Time Bound

Motion, growth, and progress are almost always measured in both space and time. Healthy spiritual goals will include a consideration of time. There is a huge difference between my saying, "I'm going to share my faith in Christ with someone else sometime during my lifetime" and my saying, "I'm going to share my faith in Christ with someone this week." The first example is a very poor excuse for a goal and close to an expression of disobedience; the second puts me into the thick of God's work in the world.

Most agree that goals should be determined for both the short-term and the long-term. There seems to be a consensus that short-term goals should be annual and that long-term goals typically cover a three- to five-year span, with a recent movement toward the shorter side of that span.

If your church had a mission statement similar to Perimeter's and included a statement related to making mature and equipped followers of Christ, you might establish the following short- and long-term ministry goals after you have reached agreement on your definition of a disciple:

- Develop a disciple-making ministry in which 50 percent of the congregation is actively involved in the ministry within five years.
- Identify, equip, and mobilize six male and six female discipleship leaders to launch ten adult discipleship groups in twelve months.
- Identify, equip, and mobilize six male and six female discipleship leaders to launch ten high school discipleship groups in twelve months.

As you can see from this illustration, there are likely to be multiple SMART goals associated with answering the question, "How will we achieve our mission?" In this example, we have identified four SMART goals related to fulfilling the mission statement "to make mature and equipped followers of Christ." There are SMART goals related to adult ministry participation, adult leadership development, and Next Generation leadership development.

Who Sets the Goals?

Though there is not an agreed-upon answer by all, I believe there is wisdom in allowing the pastor to start the goal-setting process. Time spent in prayer and seeking the mind of God should be the starting point. In a multistaffed church, other staff members should share their counsel (and have major influence in the goals that relate to their specific ministry). In an elder-led church, the elders should have final approval. As the senior pastor, my evaluation is determined in part by my performance against the goals. Thus, it is important that we agree on the goals that are ultimately used.

SPECIFIC ACTION PLANS, RESOURCES, AND BUDGETS FOR ACHIEVING SMART GOALS

Each of the SMART goals is broken down into specific action plans with timelines and responsibilities. I suggest developing schedules by starting at the date the goals are to be accomplished and working backward. As this process unfolds, you will see if reasonable time has been allotted and whether your goals can actually be accomplished. This process has helped us avoid a good deal of late and frustrating schedule changes caused by poor planning at the outset. The chart on the next page is an example of developing action plans for achieving the strategy, "Establish the process and criteria for recruiting and selecting leaders."

Another element of the operating plan is to identify the resources and budgets required to successfully implement the plans. Resources include full-time staff, volunteers, equipment, supplies, facilities, and other resources needed to achieve the plan. Depending on the planning requirements of your church, your budget would include staff salaries and benefits, equipment purchases, supplies, and expenses.

Action Step	Responsibility	Completion Date
Draft criteria for recruiting and selecting leaders	Bob Smith	June 5
Review criteria with immediate supervisor	Bob Smith and Fred Williams	June 10
Revise criteria based on agreements with immediate supervisor	Bob Smith	June 15
Review and secure approval from immediate supervisor	Bob Smith and Fred Williams	June 20
Present criteria to adult-ministry leader team	Bob Smith, Fred Williams, and adult-ministry leader team	June 25

Planning Is a Process

As you are developing your SMART goals, strategies, and action plans, you are likely to reach a point in the plan when you realize that you cannot achieve one of your SMART goals due to one of a number of reasons:

- As you map out the timelines, you realize that you cannot accomplish the goal within the established time frame.
- As you develop your budgets, you realize that you do not have sufficient budget to fund the scope of the activities identified in the plan.
- As you develop your plans and identify the people or other resources required to achieve the plan, you discover that you don't have or cannot get access to the resources required to implement the plan.

When these situations occur, you then need to go back and make adjustments to the plan. In some cases it may be as simple as revising the target date. If the project was a critical building block for achieving another aspect of the overall ministry plan, then your plan might be revised to secure additional people and/or financial resources to make it possible to achieve the goal by the original date.

One of the greatest downfalls of planning is that it produces a document that ends up on a shelf in someone's office and then isn't considered again until the next planning cycle. A plan is like a road-map that helps guide you on your journey. It is something that you should refer to on a regular basis to ensure that you're on course to achieving the SMART goals that have been established.

Evaluating Your Plans

As you design your infrastructure and develop your operating plans for making mature and equipped disciples, you will continually review everything that you do against the strategic plan (purpose, vision, values, mission, and definition of a disciple) by asking questions such as these:

- How does this particular element of the plan or process fulfill our definition of disciple and bring about the desired *transformation in* the lives of our people?
- If we are able to successfully implement the mission statements, will they lead to accomplishing our vision?
- Taken together, will the plans that we have developed fulfill the mission statements?
- Are we being intentional at equipping, mobilizing, motivating, and holding our people accountable for personal evangelism, outreach, and service in the community?
- Are the plans consistent with our stated values? Is our focus in all that we do glorifying to God?

Additional Resources to Consider

A full discussion of goal setting is simply not possible in this book, but there are some excellent resources available for further study. One that I have appreciated is James Collins and Jerry Porras's book *Built to Last*, from which I have already quoted. They have a great chapter about the importance of BHAGs (Big Hairy Audacious Goals). They claim that every organization needs at least one or two goals that are set big enough and even outrageous enough to create a sense of vision and enthusiasm in the hearts of those responsible to accomplish the task.

Such goals certainly inspire people, but for believers it is important to make sure that the motive for goal setting is that of meeting needs, not merely accomplishing astonishing results. Likewise, it is very important when setting goals not to allow them to be based upon the past or upon personal preferences. The leading of God must be the reason for choosing the goals that are set. Having said that, a healthy application of the BHAG principle brings to the goal-setting process the same kind of stretch and faith that characterizes our definition of a worthy vision—an effort of such magnitude that it is bound to fail unless God is in it!

Another helpful resource is the book *Encouraging the Heart*, by James Kouzes and Barry Posner. They note that feedback when setting and monitoring goals is critical if we expect to see them met. Kouzes and Posner cite a Stanford University study showing that goals alone result in about a 24 percent improvement in performance effort. When feedback is added, there is a staggering 59 percent improvement.[2] This is simply a statistical confirmation of the power of accountability. Staff reviews that measure current performance against previously agreed-upon goals is a fair approach to doing evaluations. Such use of goals is especially beneficial when feedback, encouragement, and development are the focus.

Notes

1. James C. Collins and Jerry I. Porras, *Built to Last* (New York: HarperCollins, 1997), 93, 202.

2. James M. Kouzes and Barry Z. Posner, *Encouraging the Heart: A Leader's Guide to Rewarding and Recognizing Others* (San Francisco: Jossey-Bass, 1998).

17

Inside the Effective Ministry Plan

10. ONGOING MEASUREMENT

KEY QUESTION

—⁓—

WHAT IS A REASONABLE TIMELINE OF SPECIFIC TASKS NEEDED TO ACCOMPLISH OUR GOALS?

We now find ourselves at the final element of an effective ministry plan. Any one of the components by themselves may seem simple and not particularly insightful. However, when taken together as a whole, these ten components hold the potential for providing you and your leadership team with a means to focus your efforts and resources on the achievement of your God-given vision.

The final component is measurement systems. How many times have you been on a family trip and had your child ask this question every ten minutes, "Are we there yet?" This question is simply the child's way of saying, "Are we making progress?"

For a church, a well-defined system of measurement and reporting provides the means to answer the question, "Are we on track for fulfilling our God-given vision?" As you work through the process of developing your ministry plan, I encourage you to identify your measurement and reporting systems just as you would any other part of your plan.

With the appropriate metrics in place, planning discussions are more productive because they are based upon empirical data rather than subjective points of view. Powers of persuasion give way to the objective data and will allow the ministry to evaluate circumstances and take the steps necessary to continue on the path of fulfilling the vision. One of my elders has told me that in his business a fundamental principle is, "You can't manage what you can't measure."

There are three key elements to consider when developing a measurement-and-reporting system:

- What will be measured and at what frequency?
- Who is responsible for the measurement?
- How will the information be reported and to whom?

As you identify key metrics for your ministry, a good test of their value may be determined by answering these two questions.

- What decisions will I be able to make from this information?
- Does the value justify the cost of gathering this information?

WORDS OF CAUTION AND QUALIFICATION

For some reading this book, you may believe that I am advocating that you should run a church like a company runs a business. I certainly understand that ministry is not business, but I do believe that the application of time-tested principles may help us increase our effectiveness at fulfilling our God-given vision.

Effective measurement systems have allowed us to maintain a record of our progress here at Perimeter Church over the years. We recognize that the growth in the lives of our people and the changes that are taking place in our community are directly related to God favoring us as we seek to be obedient to the vision He has given us. It can be very encouraging to see how God has worked through the years.

CHANGE: OPPORTUNITY FOR EXCITEMENT . . . OR FRUSTRATION

People resist change. Their resistance rarely flows from a thoughtful rejection of the proposed change itself. More often than not, people resist change because they simply don't like change. So it serves us well to know something about change management. Many of my acquaintances are laughing right now as they think about the idea of my writing on this subject. I readily admit that yesterday is too late for me regarding any desired change. I also admit that it is healthy, challenging, and maddeningly frustrating for me to help lead an organization that by nature resists change. The process develops patience in me, though I do find myself uttering that classic prayer, "Lord, make me patient . . . now!"

I would love to tell you that there is one, simple, tried-and-true method for introducing and managing change. Even a God-given vision can run into resistance and obstacles that prevent it from being executed to its fullest. While there are general principles for how to approach change, you will need to evaluate each situation to determine the most appropriate means for introducing the change. As you will learn from the discussions that follow, there are times when you will make communication of change a very public process in which the vision and changes are communicated with personal and churchwide communications in a way to generate excitement, enthusiasm, and participation. There are other times when the changes should be introduced quietly and without a high-profile communications campaign.

Because change is difficult for most people, the leadership of the church needs to bathe the anticipated change in prayer on a continuing basis. The leadership team should be praying for the change individually and as a group. If the change is being launched with a high-profile campaign, you should communicate prayer needs to established prayer teams. You might even consider establishing special prayer teams or events to support the change process.

Another key element in the plan for implementing the change is to present the circumstances that led the leadership to implement the change. There may have been a scriptural mandate or some significant shift in the environment that has necessitated the proposed change.

Managing High Visibility Changes

We are all familiar with high visibility changes that occur within the church:

- New building, facility expansions or renovations
- Relocating to a new campus
- Changes in churchwide organizational structure. For example, the church may realign using small groups or structuring congregations into geographically aligned congregations and neighborhood groups
- Planting a new church in which members of the parent church will form the nucleus of the new church
- Launch of a Christian school
- Launch of a new ministry that will require a significant commitment by staff, lay leaders, and the congregation as well as a significant commitment of budget and financial resources to be successful

Although there is no set formula for announcing and launching the plans related to these changes, the chart below provides an effectively visual representation of the change process. A thoughtful, intentional plan will ensure a higher probability of successfully implementing the change.

THE CHANGE PROCESS

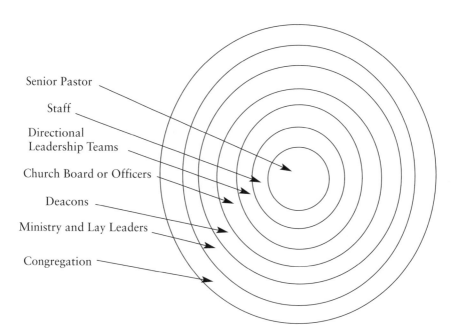

Senior Pastor

Staff

Directional
Leadership Teams

Church Board or Officers

Deacons

Ministry and Lay Leaders

Congregation

In many situations, the process generally starts with the senior pastor receiving a vision or identifying a strategy that supports the vision and mission of the church. The pastor may seek input from staff and key leaders to clarify and refine the idea. The idea is then presented to the appropriate leadership group for review and input to take the next steps of implementation.

Depending on the level of communication you want to provide, the next step is to develop a communication plan for the various "stakeholders" in the project. The objective of this communication is to communicate the circumstances that require that this change take place, seek feedback and input, and gain their support. By engaging the stakeholders as early in the process as possible and providing them with opportunities to provide input and shape the idea, they will begin to take ownership for and be enthusiastic advocates for the change.

Quiet Changes

Certainly there are times when the best change management is to simply make the change without calling attention to it. Far too often I have invited resistance by seeking to get ownership from our people when, in reality, few if any would have even noticed the change.

Because change comes so hard for so many, it is often best, when possible, to merely add new initiatives without killing the old ones. The key words are "when possible." Some new programs cannot exist alongside the old, and thus coexistence is not possible. But occasionally it is possible.

I have been told that in the bayou, where buildings are built on stilts, the wet conditions cause rapid rotting of those stilts. Instead of replacing the old ones, however, new ones are merely added. As the old ones rot and the waters move in and out, the old stilts eventually wash away. Similarly, it is often the wisest choice to allow old programs to die natural deaths while the new ones thrive.

> WE SHOULD BE CONSTANTLY EVALUATING OUR CHANGE OPPORTUNITIES AGAINST THE STANDARD OF, "IS THIS GOING TO BRING GLORY TO GOD?"

I would never advocate change for the sake of change alone. Indeed I would say that we should be constantly evaluating our change opportunities against the standard of, "Is this going to bring glory to God?" However, as we have considered this topic of change, I would be remiss if I did not place this conversation in the context of what I think is one of the most vexing problems we face in the church today. I am amazed, indeed alarmed, at the continual rise of consumerism in the church today. I have given this much thought over the years. Here are some of those thoughts (from my journals) for your consideration:

I remain alarmed at the ever increasing rise of consumerism in church. I have to deal with it nearly every day in some form or fashion. The lost world seeks for satisfaction by going from toy to toy, relationship to relationship, and fix to fix. We know that only Christ can fill the void. For Christians, many are no different from the world. Their toys, relationships, and fixes are substituted for church programs, ministries, experiences, and new biblical teachings. But only Christ, yielding His glory deposited in our lives, can fully satisfy. As a pastor, I often feel I am pressured to keep manufacturing programs, ministries, and teachings that "fill their needs" in order to keep people satisfied; and I become weary of this. I often feel like a spouse must feel when, though being a good mate, still finds his or her spouse dissatisfied.

There are so many consumer paradoxes that have baffled me over the years:

- *People want something new, fresh, and exciting but do not want change.*
- *People want to go deep but don't want to invest the relational time necessary.*
- *People want deep, interesting, relevant, and well-illustrated messages but want them to be short and simple.*
- *People want more and more services provided but resent being asked to serve in the support of those services.*
- *People want more communication but will not attend special meetings designed to provide them with more information and get fed up with mail and e-mail coming to their homes.*

And the list goes on and on.

In this context, a leader must be discerning when deciding when to initiate change, measuring the potential gains against potential losses. Most people want change without losses. But as I have said previously, when you say yes to one thing, you are by design saying no to many other things. Change always has a loss associated with it. Many leaders are so paralyzed by the prospect of loss that they are often unwilling to initiate changes even when they are critical to the ongoing success of the ministry. When the change is carefully evaluated and it is determined that the gains outweigh the losses and a majority of the people will benefit from the change, a leader must lead that change. Living in a consumerist culture presents challenges, but it does not release a leader who has been called by God, from the responsibility to lead. Even if it is against what seems to be a cultural tidal wave slamming against the church.

Over the years I have said this prayer: "God, make me wise in my discernment of gains and losses and secure enough in You to embrace the criticism that comes from leading change. Lord, thanks for the privilege to participate in leading change that results in Your glory. I love You."

MEASUREMENT AND CHANGE MANAGEMENT— WORTH THE INVESTMENT

The time that you spend in the development and implementation of your measurement plans will pay great dividends. Effective measurements will help you understand what's working well and what needs to be improved. With this information you will have direction to guide revisions to your plans.

As you read this, your initial reaction is likely to shorten or even skip the change management process. However, with this last piece of the puzzle you are now in a position to bring your ministry plan to a completed state. You can now focus on the execution and begin to experience the thrill of seeing God work in and through your people as He makes you a transformational church. In the next chapter I have spotlighted some tough choices that you will no doubt be faced with as you begin this adventure. Do not become discouraged. When God has given a vision He will also provide the means to see that vision come to pass. So press on!

18

MAKING THE TOUGH CHOICES

Designing a ministry plan is a rigorous exercise in making difficult choices. That is probably the main reason so few people attempt to do it. Consciously or unconsciously, pastors and church leaders recoil from the dangerous waters they will have to navigate in order to develop such a plan. But I believe the voyage is completely worthwhile.

Through the years of leading our church, I have come to realize that choices are difficult because most decisions create contrasting problems. Most tough choices are made on a continuum between contrasting values or priorities, and in most churches, there are fierce proponents of either extreme. Here are some of the continuums:

⟵————————————————————————————⟶
Seeker   Believer

⟵————————————————————————————⟶
Traditional   Contemporary

←	→
Single-minded focus	Variety and choice
←	→
Program oriented	Discipleship oriented
←	→
Top-down leadership	Bottom-up leadership
←	→
Spiritual growth emphasis	Social emphasis

We rarely have the option of making a decision that results only in advantages. I will illustrate using one of the continuums above: "single-minded" focus versus "variety and choice" focus.

When you think about effective evangelism, which parachurch organization comes immediately to mind? Most of us will agree— Campus Crusade for Christ. Why are they known for such effective evangelism? In large part because they are so singularly focused. Everyone in Crusade must use "The Four Spiritual Laws." No other method is sanctioned. Regarding personal methods, there is absolutely no option for variety. Regarding stylistic preferences, a staff member's choice is not considered. As a result, many people choose not to be involved with Crusade. Many are even critical of Crusade's narrowness (or perhaps, better said, its single-minded focus).

Campus Crusade has made a choice. They chose to be extremely strong in evangelism by being singularly focused regarding their method. At the same time, they chose not to regard the individual needs and desires of their constituency. They are confident enough in their track record that they don't hesitate to encourage those who insist on an individualistic style of evangelism to practice it freely on their own, outside of Campus Crusade.

STRENGTHS AND WEAKNESSES

To move one way or the other on any of these continuums is likely to create a strength, and every strength on every continuum creates its own matching weakness. The stronger the emphasis on contemporary expression, the weaker will be the appeal to those who expect and appreciate traditional expressions. A highly program-oriented organization may present a structure that fits everyone, but the quality of discipleship for the individual believer will tend to be weaker.

What makes many choices so difficult is that they don't have to be made between the good and the bad, but rather between the good and the best. The good can be the enemy of the best; and many people like the spiritual good more than the spiritual best. Churches often lose healthy morale and people if they don't offer the good, yet can lose out in the kingdom if they are not offering the best. And the church can rarely offer both at the same time. The church, therefore, will never reach its full potential without its people developing a passionate desire to seek the best, not merely the good.

ALIGNMENT

The term *alignment* is a favored word around Perimeter. Our staff director has made sure that every staff member constantly thinks in terms of alignment.

Putting *Built to Last*'s definition of alignment into a ministry context, we define alignment as making sure that "all the elements of the ministry work together in concert within the context of the church's core ideology and the type of progress it aims to achieve."[1]

Hard Questions

Alignment is not simply deciding that something is merely not opposed to one's vision. It is determining that whatever is embraced within the ministry supports and advances the vision. Thus, the question to ask is not, "Is this practice good?" but rather, "Is this practice the best for us, fitting consistently with our ideology and mission?" Another question to ask of anything being considered is, "Would this move us closer or further away from our mission and vision?"

We faced such hard questions when we had to decide whether our adult communities, which met on Sunday morning, would enhance or hinder our effort to become a TEAMS-based church. Our decision, until additional space could be built, was to reassign the space used for adult communities to leadership training for those pastoring and discipling. Not a very popular decision! But it was certainly a decision in alignment with our vision. And the limitations of time and space made the decision unavoidable. Later, in a new facility, we were able to offer the adult community option again, without compromising our primary commitment to equipping and discipleship. The more a ministry plan is understood and accepted by the congregation, the easier it is to weather these difficult decisions. When there is no clear mission and vision, anything "good" is much harder to turn away.

The Alignment Process

In order to determine alignment, it is important to define the activity in question, including the purpose, vision, mission, goals, and resources required. Then church leaders must apply the previously discussed questions: "Does this activity fit with our church ideology (vision and core values) and does it promote the achievement of our goals?" Considering all of this, it's time to make a decision—sometimes a hard one.

Add to all that's been said the reality that the modern church, specifically in America, is absorbed in consumerism. People tend to treat their personal choices as the highest authority in their lives. Submission is often rejected simply because it challenges our "right" to do what we want. This makes our choices as leaders of Christ's church even harder. People today think much more in terms of what they want than in terms of what they need, and the gap between the two is growing rapidly.

THE *REAL* NEEDS

If people were choosing a church based on what they truly need, they would be most attracted to a church that has a

- passion for God's glory,
- solid biblical theology,
- commitment to and training for disciple making,
- commitment to and training for disciple training, and
- commitment to church discipline.

However, people are usually attracted to a church that offers

- enjoyable preaching,
- inspiring music, and
- enjoyable and convenient programming.

A good friend of mine who pastors one of the fastest-growing churches in America was quoted in a national Christian magazine describing the mentality of the people at the church he pastors. He said, "We could change our theology and no one would care, but if we changed our music we would split the church."

CONGREGATIONAL PARADIGMS

So, pastors and church leaders, perhaps the biggest continuum decision you must make has to do with your values regarding which of the following two targets you would choose if you had to choose one over the other.

The first target is pictured by the diagram below:

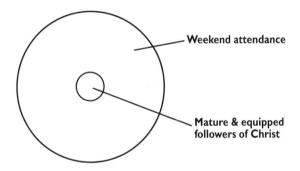

The first target is a church that is extremely popular among the community, possibly based on giving its people what they want, perhaps representing that which is good. This church often ends up functioning like Bud Wilkinson's famous description of a football crowd in a stadium on a weekend—"Twenty-two men on the field desperately needing rest, and fifty thousand people in the stands desperately needing exercise." (When Howard Hendricks tells this story, he concludes by saying, "What a description of the local church!") This model certainly fits a consumer-entertainment mentality. But does it please God?

The next diagram represents a second approach that focuses more on its people's needs (representing that which is best for the people).

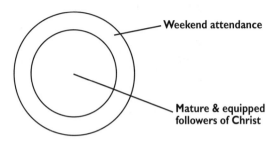

Its outer circle is not as large, yet the inner circle is considerably larger. This is not to say that the better the quality of the discipleship and ministry of a church, the lower the quantity of attendees and members. But it could possibly mean that.

Beginning with our first staff and officer retreats nearly twenty-five years ago, I have continuously kept these two targets before the leadership. I said then, and I'll say it now, there are decisions we can make that will make us a more enjoyable church yet less effective at making mature and equipped followers of Christ. My choice of targets lies clearly in the second. Ideally, we see the Lord give abundant fruit in growth (quantity) while making decisions based primarily on what will take our people through healthy spiritual formation (quality).

Paradigms and Tough Choices: Groups

When we decided to go to a discipleship-oriented ministry, the spiritual growth of a significant minority of our people accelerated measurably. However, in order to equip leaders to be effective disciple-trainers, we needed to give this training the best of our prime time and primary leadership. As I mentioned earlier, this meant that because we had limited space on Sunday morning, and limited leadership, we needed to discontinue adult Sunday school. This was a tough, unpopular choice. But we stuck by it because it was in clear alignment with our ministry plan. This decision enabled us to use our leaders and available rooms for equipping leaders who would be discipling and pastoring our people during the week. The results eventually demonstrated the wisdom of the choice.

In addition to this, we felt that we needed a more singular focus on discipleship and decided that for the first several years we would curtail other types of small groups that competed with discipleship teams for leadership and training resources.

The result was that, while the spiritual formation of our people excelled significantly, the sense of satisfaction among many of our people decreased. The prevalent feeling of many in the church over the next few years was that fellowship in the church had diminished and that life at Perimeter was not as enjoyable as it used to be.

Several years later, after discipleship was firmly rooted in our church, we were able to add other types of groups with the belief that these offerings could now serve as a funnel into discipleship (without threatening the health of our most valued nurturing ministry).

Paradigms and Tough Choices: Young People and Worship

Another example of a choice posing a challenge to church leadership has to do with the felt need of parents and their children and youth to have worship services designed specifically for the children and youth. Here the leadership members need to ask themselves, What is best for the young people? (We certainly know what their wants are, but what about their needs?)

Depending on where you land on this issue, you may have a hard choice. You may believe that such accommodating worship services are unhealthy. You see them producing high school graduates who have never been to adult worship or seen their parents worship, and who will struggle with church throughout college and adulthood because the music and worship style are not their preference. (I recently heard a reputable speaker say that youth who attend youth worship rather than worship with adults are far more likely to drop out of church when they attend college. Though I don't know his source of information, I would expect such to be the case.) If this be so, we might make a hard and unpopular decision. Such may well produce a healthier ministry among our young people, but one that is not nearly as attractive.

Until a leadership knows which previously mentioned target they would choose, were they given only these two targets as choices, double-mindedness will prevail. The problem of modernity is real and must be addressed. In other words, people in our times expect and demand that their felt needs be met. The leadership of the church must resist the temptation to cave in to every demand under the threat of departure. Yet to neglect the felt needs of people can also cause the church to be irrelevant in the modern world.

So let me say it once again: To choose to meet the unfelt needs of church attenders and members as a priority over their wants is not to choose that the church will grow more slowly. But it may. I've said through the years that if we at Perimeter wanted merely to have a large church, unconcerned about the maturity of its people, we would have made many decisions differently than we did. But be careful. Don't use quality as an excuse for not growing. Healthy churches, when located in high-harvest areas, will grow.

WHAT IS INEVITABLE

If you are a pastor who is passionate about leading a intentional church, get ready for criticism. Many in the laity will not understand all that has been said above. They will come to you with what appears to them to be the obvious answers to all concerns—but they don't understand the implications of their choices. We must. Thus, every decision regarding choice of values necessitates much prayer and counsel. Then we must stay on course as long as we believe we've made the best choice for the church. At the same time, we must humbly admit it when we realize we've made a bad choice in our position on a continuum.

When my life comes to an end, or if the Lord returns while I'm still alive, I want to know that I have been faithful in my discharge of duties as a pastor of His church. When that day comes, nothing else will matter—not the size of the church I pastor or any other human measurement of success. Until then, giving glory to God by making His bride as beautiful as she can be must remain my passion—and the passion of every other church leader. With that end and only with that end must we be satisfied.

Note

1. Adapted from James C. Collins and Jerry I. Porras, *Built to Last* (New York: Harper-Collins, 1997), 202.

19

EVANGELISM:

REACHING THE LOST
IN THIS GENERATION

This chapter and the next chapter deal with the two passions that underlie everything else in this book. Whether we look at the Great Commission in Matthew 28:18–20 or Jesus' restatement of His command in Acts 1:8, the call to evangelism and discipleship is unmistakable. Evangelism and discipleship are the squeaky wheels of the effective ministry plan. They must be greased. Without biblical evangelism and discipleship, a ministry plan is doomed to ultimate failure. The plan may look good on paper and even produce a flurry of activity, but it will not lead to a church being used by God in a transformational manner.

EQUIPPING INDIVIDUAL BELIEVERS

I believe that every church should have a plan and at least one method for equipping believers to individually share their faith. To simply expect church members to be "bringers" to church in order to let the professionals do the evangelism is to rob them of their privilege and responsibility of being soul winners. Certainly all do not have the spiritual gifts and natural abilities to make them abundantly fruitful in evangelism. Christians who do not have the gifts of giving or mercy are still expected to give and show mercy. So too, all Christians can share their faith with the lost. Their approaches will differ and their fruitfulness will vary, but all can share the good news of Christ. It is the church leadership's responsibility to make certain that such equipping is made available.

As they are adequately equipped and challenged to identify, pray for, and invest relationally in a target group (a list of individuals or an identifiable group such as a neighborhood, apartment complex, or social club), we can expect increased fruitfulness.

We have a course at Perimeter called X-PRESS Your Faith, which is offered several times a year. It is here (as well as in discipleship teams) that our people become equipped to witness.

X-PRESS summarizes and implements what we expect of our people. We explain that the X is actually the letter of the Greek alphabet named *chi*. It is the first letter of the Greek word *Christou*, which means Christ. We want to remind them that Christ must always be out front. We introduce the students to the acronym PRESS: Pray, Relate, Expose, Share, and Sponsor. During the equipping sessions we help prepare our people to do all five.

EIGHT SUGGESTIONS FOR
EFFECTIVELY REACHING THE LOST

Perimeter has developed a specific plan and methodology for evangelism training that has stood the test of time. Many pastors and leaders trained at our seminars have asked us to make our curriculum more readily accessible, and those materials will soon be available in printed form. In the meantime, let me make eight suggestions for pastors who want to see their churches used effectively to reach the lost. These are in addition to the obvious requirement of demonstrating lifestyles of mercy intent on meeting the needs of hurting people who don't grasp the love of Christ. I believe these suggestions will at least give you a framework from which to think about the role of evangelism in the life of your church.

1. *Lead your elder leadership (or its equivalent) to embrace a philosophy of ministry that makes reaching the lost as high a priority as ministering to God's people.*

I can't stress strongly enough the importance of casting the vision well and often for the value of reaching the lost. Both in elder training and in elder orientation, I underscore this value as dramatically as possible. But most importantly, they must see their pastor living out a passion for the lost.

2. *Indoctrinate your people through multiple, ongoing means as to the high value your church places on reaching the lost.*

My "best shot" at this is during what we call our "Inquirer's Seminar," required of all people who would choose to join the church. This is a weekend seminar where they can learn about Perimeter. If, after the weekend, they choose to join, they can attend our Membership Seminar and then meet with elders to be examined for membership. This first seminar is my opportunity to indelibly imprint their minds with the high value of being part of a mission-minded church. The seminar introduces the newcomer to what we call "The Three Distinctives of Perimeter Church." One of our three distinctives has to do with being an effective mission that remains contemporary to its culture. The other two include being a safe home that meets the needs of God's people and being an effective equipping station that views the pastor and staff as equippers and the laity as the ministers. During the seminar I want to sell our newcomers on the high value we place on reaching the lost.

Sermons, vision banquets, newsletters, and statement of vision and mission must continuously remind the newcomers and old-timers alike that reaching the lost is a nonnegotiable commitment of the church.

3. *Make your church services and ministries seeker friendly.*

I have already addressed the importance of making the worship service friendly to nonbelievers. But the same should be applied to all ministries of the church. It is important to evaluate everything in the life of the church, from its name to its recreational ministry, to determine whether it is not only friendly to the lost but, in fact, strategically designed to reach the lost. Until you have done this, you have not applied the principle of alignment to the church.

When we began our church it was named Perimeter Presbyterian Church, based on the commitment we had and have to plant God's church all around and throughout the Perimeter (the name given to an interstate highway that encircles Atlanta). As we began to take seriously our commitment to reach the unchurched, we inventoried everything we could think of regarding how we were postured to reach the lost.

When we looked at our name, we concluded that in our particular community, Presbyterian did not serve well in reaching the lost—only in attracting Presbyterians. Right or wrong in our evaluation, based on our belief, we changed our name to Perimeter Church—all for the sake of eliminating barriers to reaching the lost.

4. *Teach your people to answer the questions that nonbelievers are asking.*

One of the leading reasons that faithful believers struggle to share their faith has to do with their fear of not being able to answer the questions that nonbelievers are asking. To eliminate such fear, we must teach our people the answers to the most commonly asked questions.

Three such questions are:

- *How can Christians believe that the Bible is God's Word and without error? Isn't it somewhat naïve to believe such?*
- *How can Christians believe that all people, including moral and religious people outside of Christianity, deserve eternal punishment? Isn't such a belief an overstatement?*
- *How can Christians believe that of all the religious leaders throughout time, Jesus is the only way to God? Isn't that a bit narrow?*

There is a fourth question that does not raise the seeker's curiosity as much as the previous three, yet is equally important.

According to the Bible, how does a person gain eternal life?

We have discovered that putting these answers in four booklets has been a confidence booster to our people. Though during our training we require the trainees to learn the answers, these four booklets, entitled *Life Issues,* are each coupled with five chapters of the gospel of John (except the fourth booklet, which has the final six chapters). These serve well to help the seeker in a week-to-week investigation.

5. *Teach your people how to wisely create a forum to address the questions that nonbelievers are asking—preferably, by teaching them how to have multiple appointment conversations rather than to make single appointment presentations.*

For many years I presented the gospel to nonbelievers primarily using a tract. Then I graduated, so to speak, to monologuing the gospel (explaining the gospel in a single presentation). But that was years ago. I was still living among people who primarily had backgrounds that prepared them to embrace the values and even the beliefs of Christianity. I found that a monologue presentation of the gospel was sufficient. But as society has become more and more secularized, monologuing the gospel is most often inadequate. I found that after I presented the gospel and asked people if they would consider accepting Christ, the seekers would often decline, suggesting that they didn't agree with my views regarding the Bible, lost people, or Christ. I felt much like *Mayberry* deputy Barney Fyfe with his one bullet in his front pocket. I would load my bullet, take aim, shoot, strike my target between the eyes, only to see him charging me—and I was out of ammunition!

It was at this time that I discovered the advantage of dialoguing the gospel. My theology has always underscored the reality that God does the converting using His converting tool, the Bible. I have believed for years that I can never change the heart of a person dead in his sin. Now for the first time I began to see my beliefs fleshed out as God used multiple appointments in which I dialogued the gospel to change hearts.

Untold numbers of times I have seen a nonbeliever who was in total disagreement with the gospel become a faithful follower after only a few weeks of investigation.

We have developed a simple diagram that can be used to stimulate an appetite to investigate Christianity. It helps the believer and invites the unbeliever to recognize that their questions and objections to Christianity are actually quite common and can be clearly answered from Scripture. We train our people to use that tool to create a forum for such an investigation.

However, the particular method chosen is not nearly as important as is the existence of a specific method (or methods) with which church members can be adequately equipped.

6. *Model for your congregation a lifestyle of being faithful as an evangelist, humbly telling your personal stories of opportunities to share your faith.*

As the saying goes, "more is caught than taught." If we as pastors are not sharing our faith on a day-to-day basis, neither will many of our people. If we don't share stories of our evangelistic encounters (including the failures), they will not "catch" the mission or be encouraged by our example. Hearing stories of leading people to Christ is not as important as hearing stories of faithfulness in sharing the gospel (regardless of the outcome).

7. *Create periodic churchwide, culturally relevant outreach events for the sake of providing easy opportunities for your people to invite unchurched friends.*

In addition to the obvious advantages to such events, there is a not so obvious benefit that comes as a by-product—a healthy self-esteem as a church experiencing firsthand the reality of being a church that is relevant to the unchurched. The more the people see their church as mission oriented, the more they will see themselves as contributors to the cause.

8. *Create a discipleship-oriented small-group ministry that equips your people to share their faith, holds them accountable to do so, and uses a group approach to reach the unchurched (which allows the participants to focus on their spiritual gifts and contribute directly to reaching the lost).*

One of the subjects that cannot be neglected in the curriculum used to equip church members is that of disciple making. As mentioned earlier, there is no better forum for equipping and holding disciples accountable than in a small-group setting.

As a small group shares in prayer for each other's target list and perhaps even shares in relational and outreach endeavors to reach a common target group, each individual can celebrate the conversion of the lost, regardless of who actually communicated the gospel story.

Since I have used the term *target group* several times, let me explain what I mean by those words. It is a term we use to refer to a people group for which you pray and with which you invest discretionary time—all for the sake of introducing them to Christ and His kingdom.

TENNIS EVANGELISM

After moving to Atlanta, I discovered that 60,000 Atlantans were on tennis teams organized around neighborhoods, social clubs, and apartment complexes. I decided to take up tennis, in part to have a common ground with non-Christians.

After playing tennis for a few years and having targeted the tennis community as my target group, I was offered an unusual gift by a close friend in our church who was being transferred to another city. He told me he wanted to give me a present as an expression of his appreciation for the ministry our church had had with him and his family. He then said, "I want to give you a gift of prayer." I had no idea what he meant by this. He explained that he would commit to pray faithfully for me for anything I asked—given four conditions.

First, it must be something I wanted and didn't need. Second, I must be willing to pray with him for this request. Third, it must be something I believed only God could provide. And last, we must agree to tell no one we were praying for this request so as not to engineer our own answer to prayer.

Without much thought, I responded with a genuine but "impossible" request. I asked for a membership to a very nice indoor/outdoor tennis club less than a mile from where our church facilities were being built. I knew I couldn't afford a membership to this club and if I could, people would be critical of my ability to do so as a pastor. But I knew that if given as a gift, no shadow could be cast.

Within a week or so, a man in our church who was in the latter stages of a battle with cancer contacted me and explained that he had previously arranged the sale of his membership to this same club and while negotiating the sale had the idea of transferring the membership to my name, without cost to me. He asked me if I would be interested in such a gift. I immediately asked if he was aware of our prayers for such a gift. He was not. He was thrilled to find himself a part of something God was doing.

It was not long after this that I was asked by a friend if I had met the head teaching pro of the club. I had not, but knew who he was by sight. My friend encouraged me to get with this pro, suggesting that he was in great need of faith in Christ.

By the providence of God, within a week or so, we parked next to each other at the same time at the tennis complex. I introduced myself to him (but did not tell him I was a pastor) and suggested we hit some tennis balls or have lunch together sometime soon. His response was, "That would be great, but what I would really like to do is to get into one of your men's early morning Bible study groups I've heard about."

I was shocked. I asked if he knew I was a pastor. He responded by saying, "Sure, everyone around here knows that a preacher has joined the club!"

I suggested that instead of getting into one of my existing groups, that we start one at the club. He agreed to host it, secure a room, provide breakfast, and mail invitations to his buddies at the club whom he thought, like himself, needed to attend a Bible study. Within a few weeks the study began with a healthy attendance. Now, nearly twenty years later, that study still continues and there is no telling how many people have come to Christ over the years through this ministry.

God honors the intent to identify a target group and then to pray for it and to invest in it. I've witnessed this at Perimeter and in many other churches.

UNUSUAL TARGETS

I heard one pastor share the story of challenging his church members to identify a target group. When he was through speaking, a young mother came up to him and enthusiastically announced that she had identified her target group. He asked her what it was.

Her reply: "Young mothers who are potty training their children."

He wanted to laugh, but resisted only because of reading the seriousness written on her face. He asked how she planned to do this.

She immediately answered, "I plan to reserve the community room at the local library, and then put up posters around the community advertising a class on potty training. I will then get a lady in our church who has successfully potty trained her own children to teach the class—asking her to include sharing how her faith became an asset to her."

Not only was this first meeting successful, the pastor said, but because of demand it was made a permanent course. Over time, special elective classes were offered geared toward specialty needs such as potty training twins, potty training the strong-willed child, and so on. (Basically, they started a potty training university!) After a few years, this ministry had been responsible for over two hundred women becoming Christians.

SENDING OUT EVANGELISTS

The apostle Peter, writing to believers in general, offered a helpful word of direction that more Christians need to take to heart. He based his counsel on the assumption that the lives of believers would be so marked by hope that others would feel compelled to ask questions. He wrote, "But in your hearts set apart Christ as Lord. Always be prepared to give an answer to everyone who asks you to give the reason for the hope that you have. But do this with gentleness and respect" (1 Peter 3:15 NIV). First, he established the motivation for evangelism—discipleship. Disciples who set apart Christ as Lord in their hearts. Then, he outlined a question that every believer should have to answer on a regular basis: "In what ways have you prepared to give an answer to everyone who asks?" Evangelism doesn't happen off-the-cuff. Effective evangelism—what appears to be effortless sharing of one's faith—is really the product of specific preparation and openness to the leading of God's Spirit. Peter's question remains an unavoidable and haunting point of accountability: "What are you prepared to say if someone asks you about your hope this week?"

Discipleship prepares us to share hope with others. Discipleship training is the other core ingredient of the kind of believers that a prevailing church produces. Discipleship will be our focus in the next and final chapter.

20

LIFE-ON-LIFE DISCIPLESHIP:

GOD'S MODEL FOR
LIFE TRANSFORMATION

Discipleship training (discipleship) is, for the most part, a lost practice in churches today. I realize that the word *discipleship* is used in many ways and that there are many varieties (or degrees) of discipleship. But as I speak of discipleship here, I refer to the most mature form defined as "life-on-life, laboring in the lives of a few."

As I noted in chapter 19, the link between discipleship and evangelism must be recognized and addressed. Evangelism and discipleship are the food and drink of the intentional church. Healthy survival depends on a consistent practice of biblical evangelism (providing the means for people to respond in faith to Christ) and discipleship (providing the specific means for people to grow in their faith, including becoming equipped to share that faith with others). Although a full treatment of discipleship is beyond the scope of this book, I would like to at least provide what I hope is a compelling case for a thoughtful, persistent, planned approach to discipleship in the local church.

DISCIPLESHIP IMPERATIVE

The need for such discipleship becomes all too obvious when we consider the following four realities:

1. *Every believer has been or is presently living under great bondage to sin.*

This reality is taught throughout Scripture. At the fall, man lost his moral ability (not his natural ability). This means that though he can do the right things, he has no ability to do the right things for the right reasons. Thus we understand statements made by Paul in Romans 3 such as "There is none righteous, not even one" (v. 10); "There is none who seeks for God" (v. 11); and "There is none who does good, there is not even one" (v. 12). Everyone is conceived in sin (Psalm 51:5) and remains in bondage to sin until delivered from its power by the redemptive work of Christ applied by the Holy Spirit.

As sinners, we are controlled by the influences of three forces: the world, the devil, and the flesh. Paul clearly explains this in Ephesians 2:1–3:

> *And you were dead in your trespasses and sins, in which you formerly walked according to the course of this world, according to the prince of the power of the air, of the spirit that is now working in the sons of disobedience. Among them we too all formerly lived in the lusts of our flesh, indulging the desires of the flesh and of the mind, and were by nature children of wrath, even as the rest.*

Paul's words to describe "in bondage to sin" are "dead in your trespasses and sins." In verse 2, Paul describes the cause for this first by using the phrase, "course of this world." Course refers to a controlling influence, and world suggests a view of life without God. Thus "course of this world" refers to a world and life view that discounts God's presence and purpose in the world.

The second influence leading to bondage to sin is described in verse 2 as "the prince of the power of the air." *Air* refers to "unseen power." This one, otherwise known as Satan, is "working in the sons of disobedience." This term *working* carries the idea of energy, force, or power. No wonder the non-Christian is in bondage to sin!

The last influence mentioned is referred to as "the flesh." There are four common uses of the term *flesh* in Scripture. Two of them are used in verse 2. The first usage refers to that which is opposite of "spirit," and the second usage refers to the animal part of man. The second usage describes the "flesh's" dominion as "living in the lusts [cravings] of the flesh." As long as we remained nonbelievers, our cravings determined our actions. These may have been good desires in and of themselves, but they were not under our full control (i.e., hunger, thirst, pleasure, sex, the desire to attract).

The second example of the flesh control is described as "indulging the desires of the . . . mind," referring to the emotional and intellectual part of man. In other words, our minds are fallen too. Those characteristics that control man's thoughts in this condition are the likes of pride, hate, and ambition.

I think it is safe to conclude that man in his sinful condition is in a most desperate predicament. Thus, we are not surprised at Paul's concluding description of such a sinner as "by nature, children of wrath." It's not a pretty picture.

On or Off the Wagon

Using this biblical picture as a backdrop, imagine with me that you have a close friend whom you are convinced is an alcoholic. He (or she) is acting unusually irresponsible and developing patterns of avoidance. In an effort to help your friend, you confront him about his abuse of alcohol. To your surprise he admits for the first time that he is addicted to alcohol. He agrees that his addiction is going to hurt not only himself but those closest to him. He then tells you in all sincerity that he is committed from this moment on to never drink again.

Now suppose you had to bet all the money you have on whether he would stop drinking. Regardless of how sincere you believe him to be, you know good and well that he will almost certainly start drinking (probably sooner than later).

So what counsel would you give him? I would imagine that you would do everything in your power to urge him to check into a treatment center to get "dried out."

Now suppose he stays in such a center for several weeks and comes out excited to find himself no longer even desiring a drink. Assume you have to bet all your money once again as to whether he would stay dry. I believe that you would have to put your money on the probability of a relapse. Though you would have hope for your friend's continued recovery, based on statistics you would still have little confidence in long-term sobriety.

So, what would you counsel your friend now? I suspect you would encourage him to begin attending Alcoholics Anonymous meetings (or some equivalent). Once this pattern of responsible behavior becomes routine, you now have a real dilemma as to how to bet your money.

Addicted to Sin

Much like this alcoholic, all humans are addicted to sin. Not until one admits to such is there hope for deliverance. But even then one must get "dried out." Scripture refers to this as regeneration or the work of God's Spirit giving a person a new heart. Only then is he freed from the controlling power of sin. This leads to the second reality.

2. Decisions to leave sin addictions are routinely followed by relapses.

Just as alcoholics have a tendency to relapse, so do believers. There is a saying in AA, "Once an alcoholic, always an alcoholic." Likewise, believers must admit "once a sinner, always a sinner" (prior to going to heaven). Common relapses for believers include worry, bitterness, selfishness, misplaced priorities, idolatry, sexual disobedience, poor stewardship, and the list goes on and on.

Spiritual Relapses

From September through June, I meet weekly with my discipleship team. We meet only monthly during July and August. During a midsummer meeting, I asked the guys, "Using 98.6 Fahrenheit as a standard, what was your spiritual temperature the day our group stopped meeting weekly?" All indicated a very healthy reading—typically only a few tenths of a degree off the desired temperature. Then I asked, "What is your reading right now?" All but one reported a worse reading than one month previously. Certainly this says a lot about the value of being in a small group, but also illustrates the tendency to relapse into old sinful addictions. A third reality introduces us to the solution to such common relapses.

3. *Life-on-life, laboring in the lives of a few, is God's master plan for rescuing addicts.*

Ask any recovering alcoholic how he or she got out of the addiction, and the person will say, "It took a sponsor to get me where I am."

Management guru Peter Drucker has said that in his opinion Alcoholics Anonymous (AA) is one of only two social institutions in the world today that are working. Why is that? It is primarily because of their use of sponsors. Those in recovery are encouraged to find a sponsor as soon as possible, to provide life-on-life accountability as the alcoholic works through the twelve steps. During that process, they are also encouraged to make themselves available to sponsor a recent survivor.

Recovering Sinners

Likewise, with those who have experienced redemption, success in sustaining freedom from sin addictions goes up significantly when a spiritual sponsor (or discipler) is available.

Jesus certainly modeled sponsorship. He made a significant investment in the lives of twelve men and an even deeper one in the lives of three. The New Testament describes such an investment relationally in younger believers on numerous occasions. For instance, the apostle Paul said in 2 Timothy 2:2 (NASB 1977, all emphases added), "And the things which you have heard from me in the presence of many witnesses, *these entrust* to faithful men, who will be able to teach others also." He also told his brothers and sisters in Corinth, "Now these things, brethren, I have figuratively applied to myself and Apollos for your sakes, that *in us* you might learn not to exceed what is written, in order that no one of you might become arrogant in behalf of one against the other" (1 Corinthians 4:6 NASB 1977). In 1 Thessalonians 2:8 (NASB 1977), Paul revealed the secret to effective ministry when he wrote, "Having thus a fond affection for you, we were well-pleased *to impart to you* not only the gospel of God but *also our own lives,* because you had become very dear to us."

I define such discipleship as "having a life product, being intentional about imparting that life product, and doing the right things to impart that life product (truth, equipping, accountability, mission, and supplication).'' It is as we've described it, "life-on-life, laboring in the lives of a few."

I recently asked an AA participant how he got enough sponsors. His response was immediate. He said, "When you've lived in the grip of alcoholism, you know its destructiveness. You also know that you would never have been delivered from its grip without the help of a sponsor. Once you've been delivered, you can't help but want to help others experience the same freedom." It's unfortunate that many believers do not use the same line of reasoning about discipling new and immature believers struggling to find freedom from sin addictions.

—w—

SUCH DISCIPLESHIP
. . . IS AS WE'VE
DESCRIBED IT,
"LIFE-ON-LIFE,
LABORING IN THE
LIVES OF A FEW."

—w—

This same friend shared that there is also a selfish motivation for sponsoring others. He said, "We have a saying in AA that goes like this: 'You can't keep it without giving it away.'" I'm convinced the same is true regarding deliverance from sin. This leads to a final reality.

4. *Without life-on-life discipleship, we run the risk of producing immature believers, at best, and disillusioned learners, at worst.*

As mentioned in chapter 8, Ken Blanchard's book *Leadership and the One Minute Manager* helps us to understand that going directly from directives to delegation creates disillusioned learners. If coaching and support are never provided or if they are removed, the hope of healthy development is minimized significantly.

Pastors and church leaders have to choose between two goals. The first is to see their people grow in knowledge and commitment. Most leaders would be thrilled to reach this goal. But further thought causes one to realize that this falls far short of the ideal. The second goal is to see people grow in maturity and equipping.

Though the second goal of maturity and equipping is inclusive of the first (knowledge and commitment), the reverse cannot be said. The reality is that knowledge and commitment alone do not take people out of moral addictions and mental and emotional bondage. Only maturity accomplishes this. And maturity is hard to come by without the investment of a sponsor or discipler.

The church must take seriously the requirement of life-on-life, laboring in the lives of a few. The leadership of churches must begin to consider how to equip their people to be effective disciplers. In order for discipleship to be extremely effective, it must demonstrate a balance between being organic and engineered. To this end, we must understand the two sides of discipleship.

ORGANIC DISCIPLESHIP, ENGINEERED DISCIPLESHIP

Organic discipleship describes the life-on-life side of discipleship. It is Jesus saying to His disciples, "Follow Me." This is the "caught" part of discipleship in comparison with the "taught" part. It is being together, learning with the world's circumstances as the classroom and the discipler's life and experiences as the textbook (all based on the foundation of the Word of God). Such discipleship may take place on the basketball court or going together to a ministry appointment. This is relationship over a period of time long enough to involve significant life challenges for both the disciple and the discipler.

Engineered discipleship is a term used to describe the structural and planned side of discipleship. This is the intentional teaching side of discipleship. God's Word also provides the basis for content. In organic discipleship, God's Word provides answers, responses, and guidance in immediate situations; in engineered discipleship, God's Word provides preparation, instruction, and equipping for yet-to-be-faced challenges in life. Decisions must be wisely made as to what truths will be taught and how equipping will take place.

DISCIPLESHIP CURRICULUM

Some today view any curriculum used in discipleship as anathema. Most who hold to such a perspective see curriculum as a detractor from being organic (life-on-life). Certainly this could be the case. But it doesn't have to be. Using the same logic that Jesus applied when He said, "If your right hand offends you, cut it off" (Matthew 5:30 paraphrased), I too would agree that if the use of a curriculum means one will not labor life-on-life then that curriculum should not be used. But how much better to have the hand not be offensive. It is much better to have life-on-life discipleship while using an excellent curriculum. The disciples walked with Jesus and observed Him day by day. But the Scriptures are also clear that He taught them content, challenged their thinking, and explained parables. Everything His Father told Him was Jesus' curriculum (see John 7:16; 14:10, 24).

My logic is as follows. If I can only spend one time a week for two or three years meeting with a small group of guys in discipleship, I want to make sure every minute counts. I can either randomly choose what I will teach, let the guys in my group determine what I will teach, or be thoughtful and selective in what I teach. All three possibilities end up becoming a curriculum. However, I have found the latter approach to have the highest likelihood of being the most effective.

I began designing a curriculum for my use in discipleship by writing down everything that came to my mind that I thought my guys needed to know in order to live for Christ as mature and equipped followers of Christ. I then eliminated what was least important in order to have a reasonable amount of information to digest in the allotted time we would be together.

When I was in college, I challenged a handful of guys each year to be discipled. I invited them to join a group where I would labor in their lives to take them to a more faithful and mature walk with Christ. I would carefully lay out the cost, explaining that we would meet three times a week for the entire school year. Once a week we would meet to study the Word of God and to discuss the things studied as assignments during the previous week. We would also meet once a week to do evangelism together (sharing our faith in a selected men's dorm). The third meeting each week was for the purpose of socializing together. So, every week I spent one night in a setting well suited for the engineered side of discipleship and two times a week for the organic side.

When I moved to Atlanta to plant a church, I immediately began the same procedure. I remember asking my first potential disciple if he would be interested in being discipled. He responded enthusiastically in the affirmative. I then asked when was a good time to meet. He mentioned that an early morning day of the week, prior to work, would be best.

I responded saying, "Great! When else?"

He looked at me like a deer caught in headlights and cautiously asked, "What do you mean, when else?"

I explained that I needed three times a week. He answered by asking me the following series of questions:

- "Do you know that I work fifty to sixty hours a week?"
- "Do you know that I have a wife and three kids?"
- "Do you know that I travel several nights a week?"
- "Do you know that I have a house and a yard to keep up on the weekends?"
- "What do you mean three times a week?"

In that moment I realized that the real world of an adult was much different than life as a student. And, likewise, it was then that I concluded that discipleship would be much more difficult in the modern American adult world.

I have had to adapt my approach to discipleship, without compromising my values and priorities. As a contrast to two out of *three weekly gatherings* being devoted to organic discipleship during my college days, now two-thirds of a *once-a-week gathering* must be spent devoted to the organic. With only one-third of my time available for the engineered discipleship, I must make every minute count.

Now most of our time together is spent in discussion and equipping regarding what was learned on one's own during the week (as opposed to using the meeting time to teach the information that needed to be learned). Selected biblical texts for personal study and books and CDs become valuable tools to make learning an all-week-long experience and not a once-a-week occasion.

A BALANCED CURRICULUM

A well-thought-through curriculum has proven to be an invaluable addition to my discipleship efforts. However, it can be abused and thus become a disadvantage. A typical signal that a leader is "engineer bound" is the statement, "I can't get through the materials."

In my opinion, a healthy curriculum for discipleship is well-balanced between systematic theology, practical theology, and biblical theology (defined previously in chapter 15). Systematic theology gives the believer a skeletal framework upon which to hang all of his biblical learning for the rest of his or her life. The vast majority of biblical theology should be learned daily in personal devotions and Bible study. I acknowledge that some lobby for making the discipleship gathering primarily a Bible study. Though Bible study is extremely important, the goal of discipling should focus far more on equipping believers with how to study on their own than on studying a few books of the Bible as a group. Don't misunderstand me! Bible study groups are extremely valuable. But discipleship teams are designed for a totally different purpose.

If you are committed to life-on-life, laboring in the lives of a few, be diligent to keep a healthy balance between the organic and engineered functions of discipleship. When Mark described Jesus' choosing of the original twelve disciples, he included a brief statement of purpose: "And He appointed twelve, so that they would be with Him" (Mark 3:14). Yes, He would eventually send them out to preach and give them authority over demons, but first He wanted them to "be with Him." Jesus' commission to His followers at the end of Matthew specifically mentioned disciples as the product of their ministry throughout the world. The transformational church is made up of mature and equipped disciples of Jesus Christ.

Conclusion

FOR HIS GOSPEL, FOR HIS GLORY

What makes a church grow? I see many churches whose pastors love the Lord and have an exceptional prayer life. The singular, focused cause of these churches seems to be the glory of God; their theology and teaching gifts are exceptional; they are in communities that give evidence of being "ripe unto harvest." Yet for some reason these churches fail to effectively reap that harvest. Time and again the evidence is that this fruitlessness is linked to a failure to develop and implement an effective ministry plan.

Yet, even so, a transforming church is the by-product of the power of the gospel, not of outstanding ministry planning. But the two should never be seen to be mutually exclusive of one another. Every aspect of a ministry plan must be driven by the gospel. Every plan and decision should be made so as to better proclaim and live out the gospel. That's an intentional church that transforms lives.

No aspect of what the church does is going to result in people transformation or community transformation outside the work of the gospel. The gospel, the good news of Christ's work on our behalf, must not only be the focus of the church, but also its power (Romans 1:16).

Ignore this truth and church ministry becomes nothing more than perfecting technique and programs. The focus shifts from what God does to what man does. Man can create large, growing, and popular churches, but only God can create churches that bring a community into a life-changing encounter with the kingdom of God. A ministry plan designed with a focus on and a dependence upon the gospel will make the heart more excited about God's broader kingdom than will simply the size and perceived success of the local church itself. What God does in the community through the church will be celebrated more than the size of its weekend attendance or its budget.

Only when the good news is understood and embraced for what it is will the church become what God intends it to be—a transformational church.

Some of my closest theological peers may well see this book as a "how-to" book of practical steps to making a great church. That couldn't be further from the truth. I don't deny the value of practical and wise advice (in fact, I believe such is important), but only the work of God, by the work of His Spirit, can empower a church to become a transformational church.

I once heard someone say that a church must function well as a cause, a community, and a corporation (organization), and that few pastors are gifted to excel in leading their churches well in all three. This book is written with a special interest in helping those who perhaps love to advance the cause of Christ by pastoring, preaching, and teaching. They thrive on building biblical community among God's people, but may find the organizational issues of ministry a distraction and a challenge. It is my hope that all will see how excellence in the "corporate" issues of churches can magnify the strengths of their cause and their community.

God's church, embracing its rightful confession of Christ, is the one weapon against which the gates of hades cannot prevail. So let's give ourselves to the church, for the glory of God, so as to see His kingdom come on this earth even as it is in heaven.

ABOUT THE AUTHOR

Randy Pope is the senior pastor of Perimeter Church in Duluth, Georgia. Under his leadership Perimeter Church has founded over twenty churches and also provides urban ministry to the under-resourced of Atlanta. Randy is a frequent speaker for Campus Outreach and Campus Crusade for Christ conferences, and served for ten years as chaplain for players on the ATP Tennis Tour. His commitment to training disciples has led to the founding of Atlanta Seminary and Perimeter Christian Schools. Randy and his wife, Carol, have four children and live in Alpharetta, Georgia.